DESIGNED TO FIGHT,
DESTINED TO WIN

Guided by Wisdom

Denalex C. Orakwue

Wisdom Power House

Designed To Fight, Destined To Win

Unless otherwise indicated, all Scripture quotations are taken from the New King James Version of the Bible.

ISBN 0-9766631-0-4
Designed To Fight, Destined To Win; Guided by Wisdom. Copyright © 2006 Denalex C Orakwue

This book has been catalogued with the Library of Congress.
Library of Congress Control Number: 2005908223

Cover Designed by: Giles Hoover, Ospreydesign.
www.ospreydesign.com
Illustration by: Craig Hamilton, Macon, GA.

Printed in the United States of America. All publishing rights belongs exclusively to **Wisdom Power House®** AKA Wisdom Power Center®. All rights reserved under International Copyright law. No part of this publication may be reproduced in whole, part or transmitted in any form or by any means without written permission of the publisher. Wisdom Power House® and Wisdom Power Center® are subsidiaries of Denalex Qualitex®.

Published by:

Wisdom Power House
P.O. BOX 16417
Sugar Land, Texas 77496
Visit our website at: www.wisdompowerhouse.com.

Guided by Wisdom

Contents

Dedication	**9**
Aknowlegement	**10**
Introduction	**11**
1. Everybody Hurts	**14**
2. Fighting Is an Art of Warfare	**17**
3. You Can Never Escape or Outgrow Warfare	**20**
4. Identify the Enemy	**23**
5. The State of Your Spiritual Health	**26**
6. Put on The Whole Armor of God	**32**
7. Destroy the Altars of Strange Gods	**53**
8. Beware of the Enemy's Stratagem	**57**
9. Beware of the Judases Around You	**59**

Designed To Fight, Destined To Win

10. Your Enemies Come in Clusters   64

11. The Constant Pursuit of The Enemy To Destroy You   67

12. Secure Yourself Against Defeat   68

13. Nullify, Frustrate and Defeat the Enemy 74

14. Make God Your Partner   75

15. Idols of Today = Demons of Tomorrow   76

16. Fighting on Your Own Volition and Terms   77

17. Resist Enticement to Battle   80

18. The Wicked Will be Frustrated   85

19. Your Enemy Will Always Lie   86

20. The Influence of Environment   88

21. Depend On God's Strength   93

Guided by Wisdom

22. Numbers Don't Matter	95
23. Size or Status Don't Matter	97
24. The Power of Discernment	98
25. The Power of Silence	100
26. Nothing Is Constant	104
27. Live and Work by Faith	107
28. Focus on Doing Right	109
29. Victory Is a Gift	113
30. Counterfeit Victory	114
31. Your thought Life	115
32. Seek God Before Going to Battle	120
33. Made in the Image of God	121
34. Avoid Your Enemy	123

Designed To Fight, Destined To Win

35. False Prophets   128

36. Talk the Solution   132

37. The Power of Agreement   133

38. Don't Quit!   135

39. If You Can Be Bought Satan Can Meet
    Any Price   136

40. Appropriating God's Power   140

41. The Power of Consistency   142

42. Expect Supernatural Intervention   147

43. Pain Is Temporal   148

44. Destined to Win   152

45. Reject Hatred Without Hating   155

46. Beware Of Your Associations   158

47. Dare to Believe God   161

Guided by Wisdom

48. False Accusation is the Last Stage Before a Supernatural Promotion   **162**

49. Never Fear Your Enemy   **167**

50. Be not Afraid of Sudden and Surprise Attack   **173**

51. Pursue The Presence of God   **175**

52. Your Promotion is Scheduled   **178**

53. Resist the Devil   **179**

54. Protect Your Dreams   **183**

55. Make Use of What You Have   **186**

56. Defining Who You Are   **190**

57. Respect Is Reciprocal   **192**

58. Identify Your Purpose   **196**

59. Forgive Totally and Completely   **204**

Designed To Fight, Destined To Win

60. Resist Anxiety, Don't Worry,
 Be Happy   208

61. Wisdom for LONG Life   214

62. The Perfect Love   217

63. Prayer of Salvation   223

PAUSE & PRAISE (P&P)
(In truth, purity and integrity of your heart)

As you read this book, pause, praise and worship HIM whose words declared, "I will bless the LORD at all times; His praise shall continually be in my mouth. My soul shall make its boast in the LORD." "I will praise You, O LORD, with my whole heart; I will tell of all Your marvelous works. I will be glad and rejoice in You; I will sing praise to Your name, O Most High." (Psalm 34:1-2, 9:1-2). God inhabits the praises of HIS people. (Psalm 22:3). The presence of the LORD is the nucleus and the seat of freedom and power, the environment of favor, an atmosphere that satan cannot stand.

Guided by Wisdom

Dedication

To The Man of war - The Father, The Son, and The Holy Spirit, who trains my hand for war, and my fingers for battle. The LORD who armed me with strength for the battle. The LORD strong and mighty. The LORD mighty in battle.To The Spirit of the LORD, The Spirit of Wisdom and Understanding, The Spirit of Counsel and Might, The Spirit of Knowledge and of the Fear of the LORD. The LORD who gives "Large and beautiful cities which you did not build, houses full of all good things, which you did not fill, hewn-out wells which you did not dig, vineyards and olive trees which you did not plant" (Deuteronomy 6:10-11). **To HIM be all the glory! I bow down and worship!**

I waited patiently for the Lord; And He inclined to me, And heard my cry. He also brought me up out of a horrible pit, Out of the miry clay, And set my feet upon a rock, *And* established my steps. He has put a new song in my mouth. Praise to our God; Many will see *it* and fear, And will trust in the Lord. (Psalm 40:1-3)
I will extol You, O LORD, for You have lifted me up, And have not let my foes rejoice over me. O LORD my God, I cried out to You, And You healed me. O LORD, You brought my soul up from the grave; You have kept me alive, that I should not go down to the pit.
You have turned for me my mourning into dancing; You have put off my sackcloth and clothed me with gladness, To the end that *my* glory may sing praise to You and not be silent. O Lord my God, I will give thanks to You forever. (Psalm 30:1-3).

Acknowlegements

Special thanks deservedly to my precious wife Maryrose, and our children: Faith Chimsom, Saint Chimdindu, Glory Chimoma and Wisdom Chimdubem, who with me gave birth to this book. They are fellow laborers in God's Kingdom.

To my late father Dennis Orakwue, a leader I loved to follow, whose words lifted me, whose wisdom guided and inspired me.

Daniel Umejesi, my good friend, we have "fought the good fight of faith" side-by-side many times. "Many letters written not by hand, but by the Spirit."

I am grateful for the faithful support and prayers of our partners and the staffs of Wisdom From Above International. Thank you to the hundreds and thousands of people who graciously acknowledged being helped by this teaching. To many friends and family, working hard and inconspicuously behind the scene, encouraging me to bring these truths from the heart to the written word, I thank you.

I am grateful for the inspiration and wisdom of many men and women of God, who have rejected compromise and pursued righteousness and justice consistently. Your legacy will endure for many generations to come.

Guided by Wisdom

Introduction

Wisdom is the principle thing; therefore get wisdom.
Proverbs.4:7
The wisdom that is from above is first pure, then
peaceable, gentle, and easy to be entreated, full of
mercy and good fruits, without partiality, and without
hypocrisy.
James.3:17

No nation emerges from a warfare without some kind of physical or psychological scars. War promises loss of life, dismissal of liberty, and emotional destruction. Spiritual warfare is far more destructive than the ones fought on a battlefield. Spiritual warfare springs from a supernatural dimension of existence where God is in charge and Satan is in revolt.

This warfare is going on in every nook and cranny of our earthly existence. You did not enlist yourself or ask for this war, yet you are in the middle of it whether you know it or not. It is a war between good and evil, often termed the vicissitudes of life. This war can be fought only from the point of view of "Spiritual Welfare," welfare in terms of spiritual good. Spiritual warfare requires a vigorous declaration of the truth of God's Word without error.

Designed To Fight, Destined To Win

To say "there is no warfare" is to deny the truth. To ignore the subject is to lose the battle. The glib assertion that there is no warfare must be annihilated to claim the gift of victory over evil. This war involves everybody on the face of the earth. Nobody can claim any immunity. The war is fought in you and among parts of society that surround you every day. The tragedy is that many do not realize they are in the middle of warfare. It is written, "My people are destroyed for lack of knowledge: because you have rejected knowledge, I will also reject you from being priest for Me" (Hosea 4:6).

You cannot be complacent nor ignore errors in this battle. You must exterminate erroneous thoughts and ways of life by the truth of God's Word or it will prostrate you with fear, loneliness, and self-pity. With intrepid conviction of God's Word, we must reject and resist the seditious propaganda of the devil and his legion of demons that would attempt to throttle our purpose in life. With resolute fearlessness, fortitude, and endurance we must fight this battle. As God said to Joshua, "Be strong and of good courage; do not be afraid, nor be dismayed; for the Lord your God is with you wherever you go" (Joshua 1:9).

In complete reliance, obedience, and faith in God's Word, Joshua led the people forward. The Almighty power of God brought victory again and again to Joshua and his people. God will do the same for you in your complete reliance, obedience, and faith in Him. Obedience opens heaven, but disobedience closes heaven.

Guided by Wisdom

We are commanded to "fight the good fight of faith." (1 Timothy 6:12). In obedience, we must demand complete freedom from satanic influences. Freedom is never granted voluntarily by the oppressor. The oppressed must fight and demand complete freedom from the oppressor. We must fight to annihilate any satanic citadel in our minds. The order of the day is Attack! Attack! Attack! Those who attack must vanquish, those who defend merely survive, and those who are indifferent will die. To live, you must fight. Those who want to live must fight, those who want to die don't need to fight. Give the enemy no time to regroup his forces, but keep him off balance by deterministically demanding the occupied territory, physical, emotional, spiritual, or mental. The enemy must be thrown out violently. He's got to go! If we fight the good fight of faith, we will receive the crown of life.

We are not promised the victorious crown if we sit with folded idle hands. Paul the Apostle said, "I have fought a good fight, I have finished the race, I have kept the faith: Finally, there is laid up for me the crown of righteousness, which the Lord, the righteous judge, will give to me at that day: and not to me only, but also to all who have loved his appearing" (2 Timothy 4:7-8). "Do not fear any of those things which you are about to suffer: indeed, the devil is about to throw some of you into prison, that you may be tested, and you will have tribulation . . . Be faithful until death and I will give you the crown of life" (Revelation 2:10).   **(P&P)**

Designed To Fight, Destined To Win

1

Everybody Hurts

Everybody hurts! But many people are hurting and afraid to say anything for fear that they will be an imposition. If this is not your season for hurting, wait for your scheduled season - it is unavoidable. "To everything *there is* a season, A time for every purpose under heaven. A time to weep, And a time to laugh" (Ecclesiates 3:1&4).

Have you ever wondered if you are in the devil's speed dialing system? Have you ever asked what is it that the devil knows about you that you don't know about yourself? What is it about your destiny that makes hell pays a personal attention on you? What is it that makes you a treat to the kingdom of darkness? Why is the devil freaked out about you? Why does he think you must be stopped? Why are you on Satan's hit list? Truly, you mean trouble to the kingdom of darkness!

The devil is a thief and a liar who comes to steal, kill, and destroy (John 10:10). The devil is a many-sided and versatile demagogue. He is a leech and lacking in life. The only thing he can offer is death. Man is the object of

Guided by Wisdom

his schemes, his destructive devices, and his ambition. The devil is the evil one, and he brings an evil day. It is written, "Deliver us from the evil one. Therefore take up the whole armor of God, that you may be able to withstand in the evil day" (Mathew 6:13; Ephesians 6:13).

Nothing in the Word of God indicates that anyone will escape an attack from the evil one or that anyone will escape an evil day brought by the evil one. The Word of God promised victory and deliverance from the evil one and from an evil day. "And the Lord will deliver me from every evil work, and preserve me for His heavenly kingdom: to Him be glory for ever and ever. Amen" (2 Timothy 4:18). "But thanks be to God, who gives us the victory through our Lord Jesus Christ" (1 Corinthians 15:57).

Deliverance from the devil is deliverance from the evil one and from an evil day with many vices of which the devil is the source. It is written, "Fear not; for I am with you: be not dismayed; for I am your God: I will strengthen you, Yes, I will help you, I will uphold you with my righteous right hand." (Isaiah.41:10).

The devil's plan is to isolate you from God and His Word, and then while you are in solitude he will destroy you. Isolation is the first step towards devastation. Isolation in terms of separation from God is dangerous. You can be in the midst of thousands and still be alone, lonely, and

Designed To Fight, Destined To Win

isolated. But you cannot be alone, lonely, or isolated if you have a personal relationship with God.

It is written, "He who is in you is greater than he who is in the world" (1 John 4:4). One with God is a majority! To outweigh the enemy, you have to do only one thing – RUN TO GOD. That is the only guaranteed way to sway preponderation on your side. Then you will outweigh the enemy in influence, in power, in importance, and in numbers. "For the eyes of the Lord run to and fro throughout the whole earth, to show Himself strong on behalf of those whose heart is loyal to Him" (2 Chronicles 16:9). "The name of the Lord is a strong tower; the righteous run to it and are safe" (Proverbs 18:10).

If Jesus is your Lord and Savior, you have spiritual weapons of warfare at your disposal; appropriate them, and fight for your life. Acquaint yourself with the wisdom that is from above, and live victoriously. **(P&P)**

Guided by Wisdom

2

Fighting Is an Art of Warfare

Learn the art of fighting and become a master warrior. Fighting is to contend, to struggle, to endure, and to surmount the opposition, difficulty, or storm. Being made in God's image means we were created to fight. The Lord is a Man of War declares Exodus 15:3. One way you reflect God's image is by fighting against the forces of evil. This warfare demands unswerving alertness and vigilance toward the enemy's activities. You were designed to fight, but not necessarily against any human being, yet this battle connects in some way to human relationship. Satanic attacks are often within relationships.

You were built to fight, destined to win. You must fight only within the context of God's established battle plan. You cannot fight well without following God's battle plan. To win, you must not fight in your own strength but in God's. You must consistently exhibit both strong character and competence. You must adapt to godly

Designed To Fight, Destined To Win

values and live with integrity. God will serve as your Protector, Defender, Deliverer, Provider, and Guide. God will give you every supply needed to win. He will provide you with the knowledge of the opposition, the strategy to win, the resources needed to win, a plan for how to use the resources, and a detailed one to-one-communication.

The joy of the Lord is your strength. God must be the source of your peace and your conquering spirit. You must never place your emotional health in the hands of anybody, and you must never expect anyone to meet the needs that only God can meet. With proper application of God's principles, you will become an unstoppable master warrior and you can truly say, "I can do all things through Christ who strengthens me" (Philippians 4:13). You have been empowered by God; therefore, fight with passion, purpose, and perspective.

"Fight the good fight of faith, lay hold on eternal life, to which you were also called and have confessed the good confession in the presence of many witnesses" (1 Timothy 6:12). "Blessed be the Lord my Rock, who trains my hands for war, and my fingers for battle" (Psalms 144:1). "He teaches my hands to make war, So that my arms can bend a bow of bronze. ... I have wounded them, So that they could not rise; They have fallen under my feet" (Psalm 18:34&38).   **(P&P)**

Guided by Wisdom

MEDITATE

1.　There is no maturation point where warfare is eliminated.

2.　You must simply learn how to fight and become a master warrior.

3.　Fight the good fight of faith, lay hold on eternal life, to which you were also called and have confessed the good confession in the presence of many witnesses" (1 Timothy 6:12)

4.　The oppressed must fight and demand complete freedom from the oppressor.

5.　To everything *there is* a season, A time for every purpose under heaven. A time to weep, And a time to laugh. (Ecclesiates 3:1&4).

5　Those who attack must vanquish, those who defend merely survive, and those who are indifferent will die.

6　To live, you must fight. Those who want to live must fight, those who want to die don't need to fight.

3

You Can Never Escape or Outgrow Warfare

The Lord is a Man of War, declares Exodus 15:3. If the Lord your God is a Man of War, what does that reveal to you about yourself designed in the imageof God? God commanded you to be a fighter. You have been commanded to "Fight the good fight of faith" (1 Timothy 6:12). You have been enlisted as a soldier. You are a warrior and a person disigned for battle.

In 2 Timothy 2:3-4, you are called a soldier. As a good soldier, you must fight to please Him who enlisted you. Therefore you must simply learn how to fight and become a master warrior. Nobody else can fight this war for you. You cannot protect yourself from this warfare. Ignorance of this warfare will not protect you. This war is visited on you without options. It does not matter how saved and sanctified you are, you must fight or be

Guided by Wisdom

destroyed. You were born into a hostile and adversarial environment. You did not ask for it, yet you are in it. Life is a battle; to fight is optional, so choose wisely.

You cannot truly love anything without wanting to fight for it if necessary. If you love yourself, you must fight for yourself. This warfare is fought constantly and daily. The decision to fight is yours. Every decision increases or decreases you. Your life is the sum total of the decisions you make every day. The bad choices you make today will be back in your tomorrows.

Every good warrior goes into a battle extremely and seriously prepared to defeat his enemy. You cannot become too mature for warfare. There is no maturation point where warfare is eliminated. You can't quit when the going gets tough. If you quit, it's over. You will win if you don't quit. "But if anyone draws back, My soul has no pleasure in him" (Hebrews 10:38). "We must through much tribulation enter into the kingdom of God" (Act 14:22b) "These things I have spoken to you, that in Me you may have peace. In the world you will have tribulation: but be of good cheer; I have overcome the world" (John 16:33).

Conflict is inevitable. Because you live in a fallen world, filled with broken people, you will find yourself in many types of conflicts. The challenges that threaten and try you are the very tools that God uses to strengthen and mature you. Growing up is inevitable, but growing up with wisdom is optional. Growing old is inevitable, but

Designed To Fight, Destined To Win

growing old with wisdom is optional. As you fight through with endurance, you gain greater wisdom, integrity, and courage to engage in whatever battle comes your way. "My brethren, count it all joy when you fall into various trials, knowing that the testing of your faith produces patience. But let patience have its perfect work, that you may be perfect and complete, lacking nothing" (James 1:2-4).

The Lord is with you in the middle of any crises or warfare. You are never alone. The fact that you are in the middle of warfare does not mean that the Lord is not with you. He has promised, "I will never leave you, nor forsake you" (Hebrews 13:5). "For the Lord your God is a merciful God. He will not forsake you, nor destroy you, nor forget the covenant of your fathers which He swore to them" (Deuteronomy 4:31).

The Lord was speaking to you as well as to Joshua when He said, "No man shall be able to stand before you all the days of your life: as I was with Moses, so I will be with you: I will not leave you nor forsake you. Be strong and of a good courage" (Joshua 1:5-6).

Paul the Apostle said, "We are hard pressed on every side, yet not crushed; we are perplexed, but not in despair; Persecuted, but not forsaken; struck down, but not destroyed. For our light affliction, which is but for a moment, is working for us a far more exceeding and eternal weight of glory. While we do not look at things which are seen, but at the things which are not seen: for

Guided by Wisdom

the things which are seen are temporal; but the things which are not seen are eternal" (2Corinthians 4:8;17-18). Gideon thought the Lord was not with them in the middle of the Israeli's warfare and crises, but the Angel of the Lord appeared to him, and said, "The Lord is with you, you mighty man of valor" (Judges 6:12). Reader, if you are a child of God, the Lord is with you. Be strong and very courageous! **(P&P)**

4

Identify the Enemy

Your warfare is against the forces of darkness in various forms. The scripture reveals that your enemy is Lucifer, otherwise called Satan or Devil. In Revelation 12:9-10, Satan is called the **Deceiver** and **Accuser**. In John 8:44 he is called a **Liar** and a **Murderer**. In Mathew 4:3, he is called the **Tempter**.

Satan has an entire confederacy of rebellious intelligent evil spirits beings working for him. Satanic kingdom is highly structured and organized, headquartered in heavenly places. Satan is your nemesis-in-chief. "For

Designed To Fight, Destined To Win

we do not wrestle against flesh and blood, but against principalities, against powers, against the rulers of the darkness of this age, against spiritual hosts of wickedness in heavenly places" (Ephesians 6:12).

"The secret *things belong* to the Lord our God, but those *things which are* revealed *belong* to us and to our children forever, that *we* may do all the words of this law" (Deuteronomy 29:29).

You must never fight against flesh and blood, for that is exactly what Satan wants you to do. Satan wants you to be busy fighting people. You may be so busy fighting flesh and blood that you could forget who the real enemy is.

The battle sometimes connects to human relationships, yet the real enemy is Satan and his confederacy of evil spirits, not people. Your fight is against the kingdom of darkness. The kingdom of darkness is a confederate of Satan and demons or evil spirits including people who make themselves available as instruments of unrighteousness to cause mayhem and pain to others. Fighting people advances the kingdom of darkness and never advances the Kingdom of God. Satan uses people who make themselves available to him as tools and instruments of unrighteousness to cause pain to others. Refuse to be used by the devil as an instrument of unrighteousness to cause pain to anybody.

The Apostles Paul, John, and Peter all warned us to be on guard against the schemes of the evil one. Too many people are tools of destruction in the hands of the devil. These people may be influential or not, in authority or

Guided by Wisdom

not, in position of power or not. Some of these people even call themselves Christians – some in the pew, others in the pulpit. These are people working contrary to the claims and purpose of God for your life. They are always seeking to injure, overthrow or confound you. They do not want you to do what you are supposed to do. They are in a relationship with you only for what they can get out of you – they are simply parasites and blood suckers. They capitalize on your weakness to manipulates and control you, ultimately seeking your downfall and destruction. They may look beautiful or handsome on the outside but poisonous and deadly on the inside. If the enemy is using you as an instrument of unrighteousness to cause pain to anybody, the scripture says, "And do not present your members *as* instruments of unrighteousness to sin, but present yourselves to God as being alive from the dead, and your members *as* instruments of righteousness to God" (Romans 6:13).   **(P&P)**

5

The State of Your Spiritual Health

The state of your spiritual health, the anointing, and the authority on which you stand at the onset of any demonic attack determines the degree of your resistance and your offensive actions against the forces of darkness.

If you must walk in vicotory, guard your position in Christ. You must stand in the authority of Christ and His anointing. Christ means the anointed One and His Anointing. The anointing is the burden-removing, yoke-destroying power of God. Jesus said, "All authority has been given to Me in heaven and in earth" (Mathew 28:18). "Having disarmed principalities and powers, He made a public spectacle of them, triumphing over them in it" (Colossians 2:15). Jesus also said, "Behold, I give unto you the authority to trample on serpents and scorpions, and over all the power of the enemy, and nothing shall by any means hurt you.

Guided by Wisdom

These signs will follow those who believe: In My name they will cast out demons; they will speak with new tongues; they will take up serpents; and if they drink any deadly thing, it will by no means hurt them; they will lay hands on the sick, and they will recover" (Luke 10:19; Mark 16:17-18). This is the transfer of power into your hand. If you abide in Christ, which is to abide in the Word of God and live your life according to the Scriptures, and if you do not let the Word depart from you, you have the authority, power, and anointing required for defeating the enemy. If you abide in the anointed One and His anointing, then the burden-removing, yoke-destroying power of God resides in you.

To abide in the anointed One and His anointing, you must fortify yourself by doing the following:

1. *You shall love the Lord* your God with all your heart, with all your soul, and with all your mind. This is *the* first and great commandment. And *the* second *is* like it: *You shall love your neighbor as yourself.* On these two commandments hang all the Law and the Prophets. (Matthew.22:37-41)

2. Focus on who you are in Christ. Whatever you focus on expands. Renew your thought life by meditating on the Word of God daily. Focus your mind on things above and not on things on the earth. Create a picture of yourself in your mind's eye, appropriating all the promises of God. "Set your mind on things above, not on things on the

Designed To Fight, Destined To Win

earth. Be transformed by the renewing of your mind" (Colossians 3:2; Romans 12:2).

3. Be cognizant of the fact that the condition of your natural strength does not determine the outcome of this warfare. "Let the weak say, 'I *am* strong'" (Joel 3:10). "Not by might, nor by power, but by my spirit, says the LORD of hosts" (Zechariah 4:6). Be constantly aware that Angels are assigned by God to minister to you.

4. Live in a healthy fear of God. The fear of God is to hate evil. You must hold forth God's Word and use it as a standard for your daily training and preparations. Doors must not be opened to the enemy's influence.

5. Be an imitator of God and live a life of holiness, joy, peace, goodness, gentleness, self-control, love, compassion, kindness, humility, patience, meekness, longsuffering, bearing with one another, and forgiving one another.

6. Purge yourself from fornication, uncleanness, evil desire, covetousness, anger, bitterness, malice, envy, wrath, malice, blasphemy, filthy language, and anything else that does not glorify God.

7. Let the peace of God rule in your heart; Let the word of Christ dwell in you richly in all wisdom. Whatever you do in word or deed, do all in the

Guided by Wisdom

name of the Lord Jesus, giving thanks to God the Father through Him.

8. Meditate on whatever things are true, whatever things are noble, whatever things are just, whatever things are pure, whatever things are lovely, whatever things are of good report, virtue, and praiseworthy—Saturate your mind with these things.

9. Let no corrupt word proceed out of your mouth, but what is good for necessary edification, that it may impart grace to the hearers. And do not grieve the Holy Spirit of God, by whom you were sealed for the day of redemption

10. Avoid internal contradictions by raising your spiritual standard to align with the Word of God. Sin is insidious, seductive, inductive and destructive. Flee from temptations and chase after qualities that will build your character and integrity. Refuse to put yourself in vulnerable situations for temptation. The best way to avoid temptation is to avert it. When you see temptation coming, cross to the other side of the street and avoid it by all righteous means. Recognize that your old life is dead. You will have internal contradictions if you return to your old patterns. Release your old habits into the sea of forgetfulness. The preaching of the Word of God must cause you to depart from evil and do good.

Designed To Fight, Destined To Win

Any preaching that causes you to want to sin, or reinforces your sinful tendencies and condition, or that sets you in the direction of the kingdom of darkness is not of God. Reject any preaching that sets you in the direction of the kingdom of darkness regardless of how chocolate coated or sugar coated it may be, and regardless of the vessel or mouthpiece through which the message is delivered. You must protect the state of your mind and the state of your spiritual health at any cost.

11. Do not tell lies or repay someone wrong for wrong.

12. Walk in the Spirit, and you shall not fulfill the lust of the flesh. Now the works of the flesh are evident, which are; adultery, fornication, uncleanness, lewdness, idolatry, sorcery, hatred, contentions, jealousies, outbursts of wrath, selfish ambitions, dissensions, heresies, envy, murders, drunkenness, revelries, and the like; those who practice such things will not inherit the kingdom of God. **(P&P)**

Guided by Wisdom

MEDITATE

1. Success comes with passionate commitment and radical obedience to the Word of God.

2. Obedience drives back the power of darkness.

3. Disobedience makes room for the power of darkness.

4. If you must walk in vicotory, guard your position in Christ.

5. The kingdom of darkness is a confederate of Satan and demons or evil spirits including people who make themselves available as instruments of unrighteousness to cause mayhem and pain to others.

6. Avoid internal contradictions by raising your spiritual standard to align with the Word of God

Designed To Fight, Destined To Win

6

Put on The Whole Armor of God

Become unbeatable in your spiritual warfare by following the battle plan provided by God. Human plans and efforts are inadequate in this battle, but God's power is invincible. "Finally, my brethren, be strong in the Lord, and in the power of his might. Put on the whole armor of God, that you may be able to stand against the wiles of the devil. For we do not wrestle against flesh and blood, but against principalities, against powers, against the rulers of the darkness of this age, against spiritual hosts of wickedness in heavenly places. Therefore take up the whole armor of God, that you may be able to withstand in the evil day, and having done all, to stand. Stand therefore, having girded your waist with truth, having put on the breastplate of righteousness, and having shod your feet with the preparation of the gospel of peace; above all, taking the shield of faith, with which you will be able to quench all the fiery darts of the wicked one. And take the helmet of salvation, and the sword of the Spirit, which is the word of God: Praying

Guided by Wisdom

always with all prayer and supplication in the Spirit, being watchful to this end with all perseverance and supplication for all saints" (Ephesians 6:10-17). To be successful in this battle, you must utilize all the defensive and offensive armors according to the Word of God. Success comes with passionate commitment and radical obedience to the Word of God. Obedience drives back the power of darkness. Disobedience makes room for the power of darkness. You must apply all the principles of God's Word to your daily living. Principles manifest themselves even under the most unfortunate circumstances and when we have already given up hope of their influence. You must be defensive at every moment because you are always open to attack. You must put yourself under the covering of the almighty God by putting on the whole armor of God. The right caution consists in not neglecting out of laziness, indolence, or carelessness those measures that will help you to gain your aim and achieve preponderance of power.

PUT ON THESE DEFENSIVE ARMORS

1. **Loins girt about with Truth.** Stand therefore, having your loins girt with the truth. The first thing you must do to "put on the whole armor of God" is to come to the knowledge of the truth. Jesus is the truth. You must receive Him. "But as many as received him, to them He gave the right to become the children of God, to those who believe His name" (John 1:12). "Jesus said to him, I am the way, the truth, and the life: no one comes

Designed To Fight, Destined To Win

to the Father except through Me" (John 14:6). When you come to the father through Jesus Christ, you must know and live by the commandments and principles of God. You must stand for the truth at all times without compromise. You must eliminate anything that is false completely in your life. You must continually make choices that are based on the truth. Your relationships, business decision, and daily activities must be rooted in the truth. Any thought, activity or action that contradicts God's commandments and principles must be abandoned. You can't put yourself into an environment or atmosphere that foster or promote falsehood.

2. **Breastplate of Righteousness.** Stand therefore, having on the breastplate of righteousness. After you come to the knowledge of the truth and receive Jesus Christ as your savior, you are given a gift of righteousness. (Romans 5:17; 2 Corinthians 5:21). From your position of righteousness, "Put on the new man who was created according to God, in true righteousness and holiness" (Ephesians 4:24).
"Awake to righteousness, and do not sin" (1 Corinthians 15:34). "Put on righteousness as a breastplate" (Isaiah 59:17). Be careful and very wise, because believers can be forced by internal contradictions to abdicate their righteous standing

Guided by Wisdom

and be rendered powerless. You must resist sin and stand in your righteousness. Without holy living, whatever you do will ultimately be inconsequential.

3. **Feet shod with the preparation of the Gospel of Peace.** Stand therefore, having your feet shod with the preparation of the gospel of peace. Once you know the truth and have received the gift of righteousness, then you will know the peace from God. "To be spiritually minded is life and peace." (Romans 8:6). "Let the peace of God rule in your hearts, to which also you were called in one body; and be thankful" (Colossians 3:15). With the peace of God ruling your heart, you must then begin to share the gospel of peace with others.

4. **The shield of Faith.** Take the shield of faith with which you can extinguish all the flaming arrows of the wicked. "Fight the good fight of faith, lay hold on eternal life" (1 Timothy 6:12). Be tenacious and resolute in your faith.

5. **Helmet of Salvation.** Take the helmet of salvation, which is the Word of God. "As a helmet, the hope of salvation" (1 Thessalonians 5:8). "He only is my rock and my salvation; He is my defense; I shall not be greatly moved" (Psalm 62:2).

Designed To Fight, Destined To Win

6. **Sword of the Spirit.** Take the sword of the Spirit, which is the Word of God. "For the word of God is living and powerful, and sharper than any two edged sword, piercing even to the division of soul and spirit, and of the joints and marrow, and is a discerner of the thoughts and intents of the heart" (Hebrews 4:12). "Be strengthened with might by His Spirit in the inner man" (Ephesians 3:16). The Word of God is a victorious weapon. "Man shall not live by bread alone, but by every word that proceeds from the mouth of God" (Mathew 4:4).

PUT ON THESE OFFENSIVE ARMORS

1. **Pray always with all prayer and supplication in the Spirit.** Pray in the name of Jesus by the power of the Holy Spirit. The name of Jesus is a weapon. "In My name they will cast out demons; they will speak with new tongues; they will take up serpents; and if they drink anything deadly, it will by no means hurt them; they will lay hands on the sick, and they will recover" (Mark 16:17). Prayer is both an offensive and defensive weapon. To prevent surprises, watch and pray. Your prayer must be mixed with vigilance. Being off guard creates unreadiness for this warfare. Readiness precedes victory.

Guided by Wisdom

Pray in the Spirit on all occasions with all kinds of prayers and requests, watching with all perseverance and supplication for all saints. Praying in the Spirit is praying in an unknown tongue. When you pray in the Spirit, you speak mysteries, though your understanding may be unfruitful (1Corinthians 14:2,14). Praying in the Spirit is the most effective prayer. When you pray in the Spirit, the Holy Spirit helps your weak points –your disadvantages or drawbacks, if you will. The Holy Spirit, who is your helper, has access to classified information beyond your reach. The Holy Spirit prays on the basis of privileged and classified information. When you pray in an unknown tongue, your capacity to doubt your prayers is destroyed, because you do not understand the mysteries you have spoken. This is good because we have been commanded to pray without wrath and doubting. We have been commanded to "Watch therefore, and pray always, that you may be counted worthy to escape all these things that will come to pass, and to stand before the Son of man" (Luke.21:36).

"Watch and pray, lest you enter into temptation: the spirit indeed is willing, but the flesh is weak" (Mathew 26:41). "Blessed is he who watches, and keeps his garments, lest he walk naked, and they see his shame" (Revelation 16:15). "Pray without ceasing. In every thing give thanks: for this is the will of God in Christ Jesus for you" (1

Designed To Fight, Destined To Win

Thessalonians 5:17-18). "Ask me of things to come concerning my sons, and concerning the work of my hands, you command Me" (Isaiah 45:11). "In everything by prayer and supplication with thanksgiving let your request be made known to God" (Philippians 4:6). "Rejoicing in hope; patient in tribulation; continuing steadfastly in prayer" (Romans 12:12). "Pray everywhere, lifting up holy hands, without wrath and doubting" (1 Timothy 2:8). "And whatever things you ask in prayer, believing, you will receive" (Mathew 21:22). "And whatsoever you ask in My name, that I will do, that the Father may be glorified in the son. If you ask any thing in My name, I will do it" (John 14:13-14). "If you abide in Me, and My words abide in you, you will ask what you desire, and it shall be done for you" (John 15:7). "Most assuredly, I say to you, whatever you ask the Father in My name He will give you. Until now you have asked nothing in My name. Ask, and you will receive, that your joy may be full" (John 16:23-24)

2. **Preach the Word; be instant in season, out of season.** The preaching of the Word of God heals the brokenhearted, brings deliverance to the captives, gives sight to the blind, sets at liberty them that are bruised, and announces the acceptable year of the Lord. Jesus said, "The Spirit of the Lord is upon Me, Because He has anointed Me to preach the gospel to the poor; He

Guided by Wisdom

has sent me to heal the brokenhearted, To proclaim liberty to the captives, And recovering of sight to the blind, To set at liberty those who are oppressed; To proclaim the acceptable year of the Lord" (Luke 4:18-19). Jesus said, "Whatever I tell you in dark, speak in the light; and what you hear in the ear, preach on the housetops. And do not fear those who kill the body but cannot kill the soul. But rather fear Him who is able to destroy both soul and body in hell" (Mathew 10:27-28). Paul the Apostle charged Timothy to, "Preach the Word! Be ready in season, out of season. Convince, rebuke, exhort with all longsuffering and teaching" (2 Timothy 4:2). The preaching of the Word of God directly attacks the kingdom of darkness.

3. **Offer the sacrifice of praise to God continually.** Praise your way to victory. Praise creates an atmosphere Satan cannot stand. Praise dispels evil spirits. "And so it was, whenever the spirit from God was upon Saul, that David would take a harp and play *it* with his hand. Then Saul would become refreshed and well, and the distressing spirit would depart from him" (1 Samuel 16:23). "Let us continually offer the sacrifice of praise to God, that is, the fruit of our lips, giving thanks to His name" (Hebrews 13:15). Praise relocates the focus from you and back on God, who is your power and your ideal environment. When you are in your ideal environment, the wisdom and power

Designed To Fight, Destined To Win

of God will show up strong on your behalf, and your midnight will turn into daylight, your darkness into light, your lack into abundance. The wisdom and power of God guarantees you wealth, favor, health, success, greatness, prosperity, and all the blessings promised in the Word of God.

The presence of God is an environment of favor. One day of favor can be worth a lifetime of labor. Favor can restore in one day what a lifetime of labor cannot achieve. There is power in your praise. When your praises goes up, the power of God comes down to your level. "Out of the mouth of babes and nursing infants You have ordained strength, because of your enemies, that you may silence the enemy and the avenger" (Psalm 8:2). "Jesus said to them, Yes; have you never read, Out of the mouth of babes and nursing infants You have perfected praise?" (Mathew 21:16). Jesus verifies that the strength God has ordained for us is PRAISE. God inhabits the praises of His people. "But you are holy, O thou that inhabits the praises of Israel" (Psalm 22:3 KJV).

When Paul and Silas were wrongly accused (and imprisoned) of preaching insurrection against Rome, at midnight Paul and Silas prayed and sang praises unto God, and the prisoners heard them. And suddenly there was a great

Guided by Wisdom

earthquake, so that the foundations of the prison were opened, and every prisoner's bands were loosed. (Acts.16:15-18, 25-26). When the power of God shows up on your behalf, that power will rescue you and liberate the prisoners around you. It will set free those who are in bondage around you. The power of God in you brings freedom, first to you and then to all those within the sphere of your influence.

God gave Jehoshaphat, king of Judah, victory over his enemies when he organized a praise session. "He appointed those who should sing to the LORD, and those who should praise the beauty of HIS holiness, as they went out before the army, and were saying; Praise the LORD, for HIS mercy endures for ever. Now when they began to sing and to praise, the LORD set ambushes against the people of Ammon, Moab, and mount Seir, who had come against Judah; and they were defeated" (2 Chronicles 20:21-22). "Sing aloud to God our strength: make a joyful shout to the God of Jacob" (Psalm 81:1).

The devil is the accuser of the brethren. "For the accuser of our brethren, who accused them before our God day and night, has been cast down" (Revelation 12:10). The devil specializes in accusations. He accuses us continually before God day and night. Even so do all human demonic agents he uses against us. Every

Designed To Fight, Destined To Win

offending Christian or non-Christian is an agent of the devil. Take notice of those the enemy uses constantly against you and avoid them. Most of these agents are obvious, but some of them call themselves believers. Be very careful because some of the so-called believers pretend to have one foot in God's kingdom but are actually members of the kingdom of darkness. You shall know them by their fruits. "Now I urge you, brethren, note those who cause divisions and offences, contrary to the doctrine which you have learned, and avoid them" (Romans 16:17).

One of the weapons against accusation is praise. Praise nullifies the accusation of the devil. Praise silences the devil. Praise is a form of testimony and allegiance. When the devil accuses us, our praises nullifies his accusations. "Let the saints be joyful in glory: Let them sing aloud on their beds. Let the high praises of God be in their mouth, and a two edged sword in their hand; To execute vengeance on the nations, And punishments upon the people; To bind their kings with chains, and their nobles with fetters of iron; To execute on them the written judgment: This honor have all His saints. Praise the Lord! (Psalm.149:5-9). Praises and the Word of God executes vengeance and punishment upon the enemy. Praises to the Lord terrifies the devil. The devil was the praise and worship leader in the Kingdom of God before

Guided by Wisdom

he was demoted and permanently sacked and dethroned. "He has put a new song in my mouth - Praise to our God: many will see it and fear, And will trust in the Lord" (Psalm 40:3)

4. Overcome the Devil by the Blood and by your Testimony

"And they overcame him by the **Blood of the Lamb**, and by the **Word of their Testimony**, and they did not love their lives to the death" (Revelation 12:11).

THE BLOOD

1. Life of the flesh is in the blood, and the blood makes atonement for the soul. (Leviticus 17:11). Judgment is legally avoided because of the blood. "All things are purified with the blood, and without shedding of blood there is no remission" (Hebrews 9:22). The blood stops the destroyer. "When I see the blood, I will pass over you, and the plague shall not be on you to destroy you" (Exodus 12:13). We overcome by declaring the power in the blood of Jesus Christ. Sprinkle the blood of Jesus by faith over yourself and your household. See Hebrews 9:16-22.

2. The blood speaks. The blood of Jesus speaks for you today. "The voice of your brother's blood cries out to Me from the ground" (Genesis 4:10). "The blood of sprinkling that speaks better things than that of Abel"

43

Designed To Fight, Destined To Win

(Hebrews 12:24). "There are three that bear witness on earth; the Spirit, the water, and the blood: and these three agree as one" (1 John 5:8). God heard and responded to the blood of Abel against Cain his brother. How much more will God respond to the blood of His own Son Jesus Christ against your enemy?

- **In (1John 1:7)** – The blood of Jesus Christ cleanses us from all sin.
- **In (Hebrews 13:12)** - Jesus sanctified us with His own blood.
- **In (Romans 3:25)** - We have faith in His blood to declare His righteousness for the remission of sins.
- **In (Revelation 1:5)** – Jesus washed us from our sins in His own blood.
- **In (1Peter 1:2)** – We are elected according to the foreknowledge of God the Father, through sanctification of the Spirit, to obedience and sprinkling of the blood of Jesus Christ.
- **In (1 Peter 1:18-19)** – We are redeemed with the precious blood of Christ.
- **In (Colossians 1:20)** – We have peace through the blood of his cross, by Him to reconcile all things to Himself.
- **In (Ephesians 1:7) – We** have redemption through His blood, the forgiveness of sins, according to the riches of his grace.
- **In (1Corinthians 11:25-26)** – This cup is the new testament in my blood. This do as often

Guided by Wisdom

as you drink it, in remembrance of Me. For as
often as you eat this bread, and drink this cup,
you proclaim the Lord's death till He comes.
This is very powerful, because anytime we eat
this bread and drink this cup, we are testifying
of Jesus Christ, proclaiming the Lord's death
till He comes, and overcoming the devil.
Jesus has freed us from our sins by His blood,
and made us kings and priests to serve God
his Father (see Revelation.1:5-6).

WORD OF YOUR TESTIMONY

Testimony is a public profession of the truth of
God's Word as revealed by the Holy Spirit and
evidenced in our lives. Testimony is "witnessing"
or "being a witness." We are overcoming the
devil every time we testify.
We therefore give our lives for the cause of
Christ. "For the Testimony of Jesus Christ, For
the Testimony of Jesus is the Spirit of Prophecy"
(Revelation 1:9;19:10). "I will give power unto
my two witnesses and they shall prophesy"
(Revelation 11:3). Notice that "prophesy" here is
the testimony of Jesus Christ, according to
Revelation 19:10. Remember that Jesus promised
that the Spirit of truth will guide us into all truth
and will show us things to come. "However, when
He, the Spirit of truth, has come, He will guide
you into all truth: for He will not speak on his
own authority, but whatsoever He hears He will
speak and He will tell you things to come" (John

45

Designed To Fight, Destined To Win

16:13). The Holy Spirit testifies of Jesus. (see John.15:26).

It is not recorded anywhere in the Scriptures that the Holy Spirit will testify of Himself, or of me, or of you. He will only testify of Jesus Christ. This is very important because we need to understand what testimony truly means. It is written, "I am Your servant; give me understanding, that I may know your testimonies." (Psalm 119:125).   There is a serious misapprehension and false conception of what testimony means as revealed in the Scriptures from Christendom. Much of what Christendom calls testimony is not testimony. The Holy Spirit will not speak of himself, but whatever He will hear, that shall He speak. This same Holy Spirit lives inside us. "Do you not know that your body is the temple of the Holy Spirit who is in you, whom you have from God, and you are not your own?" (1 Corinthians 6:19). This means that the Holy Spirit will testify of Jesus through us, and we are witnesses.

We are the witnesses, and the Holy Spirit witnesses with us who are the witnesses. This is a synergistic endeavor between us and the Holy Spirit. The witnesses will testify of Jesus Christ. "And it is the Spirit who bears witness,

Guided by Wisdom

because the Spirit is truth. The Spirit Himself bears witness with our spirit that we are the children of God, And if children, then heirs; heirs of God, and joint heirs with Christ, if indeed we suffer with Him, that we may also be glorified together" (1John 5:6; Romans 8:16-17). If the Holy Spirit does not bear witness with your spirit, your testimony will not stand in the court of the Kingdom of God. Any testimony that contradicts the Word of God is a lie. The Word of God is the truth. Therefore, "Do not boast and lie against the truth" (James 3:14). Remember, Jesus is your Lawyer (attorney or advocate) in the Kingdom of God. He will defend you based on His finished work on your behalf. "We have an advocate with the Father, Jesus Christ the righteous. Sitting at the right hand of the POWER. Sitting at the right hand of God" (1 John 2:1; Mark 14:62; Colossians 3:1). Be wise in your conversation and give no place to the devil. "Who is a wise and endued with knowledge among you? Let him show out of a good conversation his works with meekness of wisdom" (James 3:13 KJV).

For example the Word of God says, "By His stripes we are healed" (Isaiah 53:5). Your testimony must also say, "By His stripes I am healed," regardless of your present challenges or how you feel. The Word of God supercedes your challenges and your feelings. All you have to do is simply agree with what the BLOOD did

Designed To Fight, Destined To Win

concerning your total and absolute redemption and freedom from the curse. "Let the redeemed of the Lord say so, whom He has redeemed from the hand of the enemy" (Psalm 107:2). When you agree with what the Word says about you, your challenges and feelings must soon agree with the word of God. Your challenges and feelings have no options but to agree with the truth once you yourself choose to do so. We have been redeemed from the dominion of sin and death. "For sin shall not have dominion over you, for you are not under law but under grace. Knowing this that our old man was crucified with Him, that the body of sin might done away with, that we should no longer be slaves of sin. (Romans 6:14,9). Our testimony must agree with the Word of God. Any testimony that does not agree with the Word of God is not a testimony. We must TESTIFY according to the revelation of the Holy Spirit. We must testify both to the Jews, and also to the Greeks, have repentance toward God, and faith toward our Lord Jesus Christ. And of the word of His grace (see Acts 20:21; 14:3). We must also testify that the Father sent the Son to be the Savior of the world. (see 1 John 4:14); that God raised up Christ (1 Corinthians 15:15); that he that believes on the Son of God has witness in himself, and he that believes not God has made Him a liar, because he believes not the record that God gave of His Son (1John 5:10); that God has given to us eternal life, and this life is in His Son (see 1 John 5:11). We

Guided by Wisdom

have to testify and preach the Word of the Lord (see Acts.8:25); We have to testify that through the blood of Jesus we have been redeemed from the curse of the law (see Galatians 3:13). We have been redeemed from the curse of poverty, we have been redeemed from the curse of sicknesses and diseases, and we have been delivered from the kingdom of darkness and translated into the Kingdom of God's Son, Jesus Christ. We have been forgiven, we have been cleansed, we have been made righteous, and we have been sanctified. Therefore, we prosper in our health, in our souls, in our finances, in our ministries, and in every area of our life.

We overcome the devil by testifying to the provisions of the blood of Jesus Christ. We have been called to be witnesses. Our very life is a witness. Our conduct and character bears witness. We must realize that Holy Spirit is the source of effective testimony. The Spirit of God empowers and enables us who believe in Him. Faith in the power of God's Spirit overcomes mountainous obstacles. "Not by might nor by power, but by my Spirit, says the LORD of host" (Zechariah 4:6). "But you shall receive power, when the Holy Spirit has come upon you: and you shall be witnesses to Me in Jerusalem, and in all Judea and Samaria, and to the end of the earth" (Acts 1:8). "You are my witnesses, says the LORD, And my servant whom I have chosen: that you may know

Designed To Fight, Destined To Win

and believe Me, and understand that I am He. Before me there was no God formed, nor shall there be after Me" (Isaiah 43:10-12). We are called to be witnesses that our God is the only God, and besides Him, there is no other Savior. We are called to be witnesses of the Word of God and the blood of Jesus. To become a witness, you must first qualify. You can only qualify by receiving power when the Holy Spirit has come upon you (Act 1:8). "But as many as received Him, to them He gave the right to become children of God, even to those who believe in His name: Who were born, not of blood, nor of the will of the flesh, nor of the will of man, but of God" (John 1:12-13). To become a witness, you must be acquainted with the power of God; otherwise, how can you be a witness to what you do not know. **(P&P)**

Guided by Wisdom

PAUSE AND PRAISE

(P&P)

Bless the Lord, O my soul;
And all that is within me, bless His Holy
name!
Bless the Lord, O my soul,
And forget not all His benefits:
Who forgives all your iniquities,
Who heals all your diseases,
Who redeems your life from destruction,
Who crowns you with lovingkindness and tender
mercies,
Who satisfies your mouth with good things,
So that your youth is renewed like the eagle's.
(Psalm 103:1-5)

"Great peace have those who love Your law, and
nothing causes them to stumble"
(Psalm 119:165).

I judge HIM faithful who has promised. "HE is
faithful that promised" (Hebrews 10:23b).

<u>Designed To Fight, Destined To Win</u>

MEDITATION

1. Your weakness is always the entry point for strange gods and demonic spirits.

2. The presence of God is an environment of favor.

3. Faith in the power of God's Spirit overcomes mountainous obstacles.

Guided by Wisdom

7

Destroy the Altars of Strange Gods

When false gods exit your life, the Truth, the Living and Holy God, enter. False gods introduce error and disorder, while the Holy God introduces truth and order. False gods will always connect you with the wrong person or people and separate you from the right person or people. Your weakness is always the entry point for strange gods and demonic spirits. Hell will always assign somebody to fuel and strengthen your weakness. When Satan wants to destroy you, he will send someone to do his dirty work.

Sometimes the person sent may be you. Think about that. Satan sent Judas to kill himself by suicide. He sent Delilah to destroy Samson. "You cannot drink from the cup of the Lord and from demonic cup at the same time: you cannot partake of the Lord's Table and of demonic table at the same time" (1 Corinthians 10:21). Any area of your life that is not fully submitted to the Lord is a crack

Designed To Fight, Destined To Win

through which the enemy will eventually attack and destroy you. "Therefore submit to God. Resist the devil and He will flee from you. Draw near to God and He will draw near to you. Cleans your hands, you sinners; and purify your heart, you double-minded" (James 4:7-8). Disobedience destroyed Achan. Anger stopped Moses from reaching the desired destination - the promise land. Greed destroyed Judas. Lust destroyed Samson. God prevented David from building the Temple because of adultery and bloodshed. Disobedience sent Jonah to the belly of the fish. Ananias and Sapphira went to an early grave because of a lie. Miriam suffered leprosy and Aaron death because of racism. **Your movement toward order will expose the idols in your life. The idol you fail to destroy will eventually destroy you.** Any movement towards order will expose something or someone that is unnecessary in your life. The atmosphere you create determines what you attract.

False gods brings curses to your life, but the true and Holy God brings blessings to your life. When the Israelites joined in worshiping the Baal of Peor, a plague destroyed 24,000 men. When atonement was made, the plague ceased, and blessings came to Phinehas and his descendants for making atonement for the people of Israel (Numbers 25.1-16). When Jehu destroyed the prophets of Baal, the Lord said to him, "Because you have done well in doing what is right in My sight, and have done to the house of Ahab all that was in My heart, your sons shall sit on the throne of Israel to the fourth generation" (2 Kings 10:30). It was counted to the credit

Guided by Wisdom

of King Asa that he was good and right in the eyes of God because he annihilated false gods. "Asa did what was good and right in the eyes of the Lord his God: For he removed the altars of the foreign gods and the high places, and broke down the sacred pillars and cut down the wooden images. He commanded Judah to seek the Lord God of their fathers, and to observe the law and the commandment. He also removed the high places and the incense altars from all the cities of Judah and the kingdom was quiet under him" (2 Chronicles 14:2-5).

What is taking the place of God in your life? An idol is anything that becomes more important than God in your life. If your life would be absolutely hopeless without a particular person or thing, then that person or thing has become an idol to you. What have you made an idol in your life? The way you live reveals your true beliefs. Instead of finding comfort in all your stuff, find your comfort in God. Let your life reflect the beauty and majesty of God. Exterminate false gods in your life and be blessed. "If the Lord is God, follow Him: but if Baal, follow him" (1 King 18:21). **(P&P)**

Designed To Fight, Destined To Win

MEDITATION

1.   Not everyone who is friendly is a friend.

2.   The Judases have neither moral rectitude nor testicular fortitude. They are unfriendly friends, disguised as friends.

3.   Anyone that changes facts about you to weaken your credibility with others is an enemy

4.   The presence of an enemy forces the Judases around you to reveal themselves.

5.   The wise man learns more from his enemies than a fool from his friends.

6.   When you know who you are in Christ, you can step into the battlefield courageously and execute God's strategic plans victoriously.

Guided by Wisdom

8

Beware of the Enemy's Stratagem

When you know the enemy, when you know who you are in Christ, and when you know God, you need not fear the result of a million battles. When you know who you are in Christ, you can step into the battlefield courageously and execute God's strategic plans victoriously. "So the great dragon was cast out, that serpent of old, called the Devil and Satan, who deceives the whole world; he was cast to the earth, and his angels were cast out with him " (Revelation 12:9). Satan is your greatest enemy, but he will not tell you so. Satan uses deceptions, lies and manipulation to get you to meet legitimate or illegitimate needs and desires through ungodly means with harmful consequences. You must therefore guard your needs and desires especially those needs and desires that are repeatedly under satanic attack. The devil can speak to you through people, sometimes as agents of offense. The devil can suggests or shows you urgent opportunity with concealed snares that must be acted upon quickly hoping to entrap you. He wants you

Designed To Fight, Destined To Win

to act immediately before you have the time to think through your decisions. At other times he could be very slow and subtle. Be mindful of his strategies. Remember that patience is a weapon that forces deception to reveal itself. Satan comes as an angel of light, a counterfeiter of God's truth. He has several objectives including:

1. *Tempt you to doubt the word of God.* God craves to be believed and hates to be doubted. Doubting God is dreadful; doubt separates people from God. Doubt gives your enemy confidence against you. Doubt kills your faith. It is like a poison, disintegrating personal relationship with God.

2. *Distract you from walking in the spirit, as admonished in the word of God.* "I say then, Walk in the spirit, and you shall not fulfill the lust of the flesh. … If we live in the Spirit, let us also walk in the Spirit" (Galatians 5:16,25). The enemy will always attempt to break your focus with anything that will derail your God given assignment, the very purpose of your life. Disruption, delays, and broken focus is sign that you are under satanic attack. Broken focus is the enemy's goal for attacking you.

3. *Attempt to disable you in the Lord's service* through sin, disappointments, guilt, and reminding you of your past sinful life.

4. *Attempts to destroy your usefulness physically and or emotionally.*

Guided by Wisdom

5. *Attempts to ruin the image of God in you.*
6. *Attempt to destroy your testimony.*

7. *Attempt to destroy and disunite Christian family.*

8. *Attempt to destroy your ministry.* **(P&P)**

9

Beware of the Judases Around You

The presence of an enemy forces the Judases around you to reveal themselves. The Judases work undercover. They are undercover agents. To successfully fight this battle, you must recognize your Judases. The Judases around you will betray you behind your back, not because you have done anything wrong, but because of their wicked and evil disposition. Judas Iscariot said, "I have sinned by betraying innocent blood," to which the enemy immediately said, "What is that to us? You see to it" (Mathew.27:4).

Designed To Fight, Destined To Win

The enemy is only using the Judases, and does not care about their destruction. The Judases have neither moral rectitude nor testicular fortitude. They are weak, spineless, and intimidated before fools in authority or anybody in a position to feed their greed. The wise in authority recognize the Judases and do not deal with them. The Judases would attempt to weaken your influence with others through their words, their actions, and conduct.

Never put too much trust in your friends and associates. Not everyone who is friendly is a friend. People can be friendly, but not friends. The Judases play two parts: in your presence, a friend; in the presence of your enemy a friend. They are unfriendly friends, disguised as friends. Be careful; not everyone who is friendly is a friend. People can be friendly to you, yet they are not your friend. Satan came to Jesus as a friend during His fast, yet he was an enemy. The Judases may show up at first with what seems like a friendly conversation, but their end game is to cause discouragement, dissolution, disorganization, depression, despair, despisement, despiritualization, oppression, rejection, grief, shame, guilt, anxiety, stress, decapitation, and even death. The nature of the Judases is to deceive with a little bit of truth-just enough truth to trick you into deception. Beware of the Judases around you. The Holy Spirit will warn you about them. Do not ignore the warnings. Jesus knew about Judas Iscariot; you should know about your Judases. (see Mathew 26:23-25).

Guided by Wisdom

The diabolic nature, meanness, and sordidness of the Judases make them habitable by demonic forces that will eventually destroy them. Your Judases will be quickly exposed when an enemy links with them. Do not be afraid of both of them. When the Judases are revealed, you are only three days away from the resurrection of another facet of your life and a future full of the promises of God. Be cool, calm, collected, and calculated. The Judases will eventually destroyed themselves. It is a law! "But woe to that man by whom the Son of man is betrayed! It would have been good for that man if he had not been born.... Then he (*Judas Iscariot*) threw down the pieces of silver in the temple, and departed, and went and hanged himself" (Mathew 26:24, 27:5).   **(P&P)**

Designed To Fight, Destined To Win

MEDITATION

1. Do not simplify the reality of the presence of Satan and his demons

2. People choose to go through the darkness of evil by ignorance.

3. Behind every ignorance is pain.

4. If you pass through darkness once, you will appreciate the light.

5. The refusal to learn the lessons of experience culminates in repeated disappointments and failures.

6. Ignorance vanishes when wisdom comes in.

7. Wisdom can be learned and applied.

8. Wisdom unapplied is worst than ignorance.

9. People who are unwilling to lose in life always win.

10. Your unwavering faith will make a declaration that will resonate and reverberate beyond the confines of your present circumstances to the spiritual world.

Guided by Wisdom

11.   God is your invincible, victorious combat partner!

12.   Never put too much trust in your friends and associates.

10

Your Enemies Come in Clusters

Your enemies are people with wicked and evil dispositions operating under demonic influences unwittingly, unleashing diabolical acts engineered by demonic forces. They will leave no stone unturned to undermine your influence. They will lyingly assail your moral character. Anyone that changes facts about you to weaken your credibility with others is an enemy. Behind every evil person and every evil act lurks the real enemy – the devil. "For the mouth of the wicked and the mouth of the deceitful have opened against me. They have also surrounded me with words of hatred, And fought against me without cause. They have rewarded me evil for good, and hatred for my love" (Psalm 109:2; 3,5). "Indeed, they shall surely assemble, but not by Me: Whosoever assembles against you shall fall for your sake. No weapon formed against you shall prosper; and every tongue which rises against you in judgment you shall condemn. This is the heritage of the servants of the Lord,

Guided by Wisdom

and their righteousness is from Me, says the Lord" (Isaiah 54:15-17).

God bears with the wicked, but not forever. Whoever rewards evil for good, evil will not depart from their house. "God is angry with the wicked every day" (Psalm 7:11). In Mathew Chapter 12, the Pharisees plotted to attack and destroy Jesus for doing good deeds. In 1 Samuel Chapter 19 Saul plotted to attack and destroy David for doing good deeds. In Genesis 37, Joseph's brothers plotted to attack and destroy him for doing good deeds. Clearly, it is the nature of your enemy to attack you for doing good and for the favor of God in your life. The enemy is not attacking you because of anything wrong in you, but rather for the good that is in you. The only way to fight back is to put on the whole armor of God, operate in the wisdom that is from God, and display a life of integrity in the face of injustice.

Never fight back with the arm of the flesh because the battle is not yours, but the Lord's. "Do not be afraid nor dismayed because of this great multitude, for the battle is not yours, but God's" (2 Chronicles 20:15). Joseph learned hard lessons after suffering betrayal and false accusation from evil and wicked people. At last when Joseph reflected on his life of betrayal and repeated injustices against him, he could trace God's hand over his life. Joseph said to his brothers who had betrayed him, "But as for you, you meant evil against me; but God meant it for good, in order to bring it about as it is this day, to save many people alive" (Genesis 50:20).

Designed To Fight, Destined To Win

Some people may come into your life with an appearance of good character, only to be shown later to have had very bad intentions and motives from the very beginning. These are wolves functioning with evil intent to wreak havoc in your life. Put every experience in the database of your memory only to learn from them later. The wise man learns more from his enemies than a fool from his friends. Forgive your enemies but never allow their wickedness. "Love your enemies, bless those who curse you, do good to those who hate you, and pray for those which spitefully use you and persecute you, that you may be the sons of your Father which is in heaven: for he makes his sun rise on the evil and on the good, and sends rain on the just and on the unjust. For if you love those who love you, what reward have you? Do not even the tax collectors do the same? And if you greet your brethren only, what do you do more than others? Do not even the tax collectors do so? Therefore you shall be perfect, just as your Father in heaven is perfect" (Mathew 5:44-48).   **(P&P)**

11

The Constant Pursuit of The Enemy To Destroy You

The enemy and his forces are relentless in their pursuit to destroy you. The enemy will stop at nothing to undermine God's plan and purpose in your life. Do not simplify the reality of the presence of Satan and his demons. The devil does a very good job being a devil. Do not take him lightly. He is no joking matter; don't be fooled. While Satan's power is limited, he is real and powerful. This is not empty or boastful allusion. Be on the alert. "Be sober; be vigilant; because your adversary the devil walks about like a roaring lion, seeking whom he may devour: The enemy roars to whittle down your spiritual resolve. Resist him steadfast in the faith, knowing that the same sufferings are experienced by your brotherhood in the world. But may the God of all grace, who hath called us to his eternal glory by Christ Jesus,

Designed To Fight, Destined To Win

after that you have suffered a while, perfect, establish strengthen, and settle you" (1 Peter 5:8-10).   **(P&P)**

12

Secure Yourself Against Defeat

The power is in your hand to coronet or depose the enemy in your life. Far too many people open themselves up for attack by the enemy by frequenting places and doing things God never intended them to do. Consequently, they are out-foxed, out-flanked, tripped, and stripped. You cannot get into a foxhole and dine with the enemy without expecting an attack. Be armored against all powers of evil. To secure yourself against defeat, you must understand the nature purpose and intent of evil. Evil breeds evil. Evil intends to destroy. Evil has an in-built multiplication factor. Ignorance increases the multiplication factor of evil. The refusal to learn the lessons of experience culminates in repeated disappointments and failures. If you must not remain in continual disappointments and failures, you must be willing to replace ignorance with wisdom.

Guided by Wisdom

When the wisdom of God comes in, your life will be translated from the kingdom of strife to the kingdom of love, from the kingdom of darkness to the kingdom of light, from the kingdom of stress to the kingdom of peace, from the kingdom of pain and sorrow to the kingdom of joy and blessing. You get the idea ?

Seek wisdom and pursue it. A decision not to seek wisdom is a decision to remain ignorant. To remain ignorant is to be subject to evil. Behind every ignorance is pain. People choose to go through the darkness of evil by ignorance. If you pass through darkness once, you will appreciate the light. Ignorance vanishes when wisdom comes in. Wisdom can be learned and applied. Wisdom unapplied is worst than ignorance.

Wisdom requires you to put on the garment of the perfect law of God. To do that, you must render the soil of your soul infertile for evil, and fertile for good. Determine to ignore and starve voices of temptation forever. Ignore them and live them unheeded, unconditionally abandoned and allowed to perish through starvation. Yes you can starve evil out of your life. Eradicate sin and impure desire in your life, knowing that there is no such thing as a penalty-free sin. The inevitable consequence of sin is penalty otherwise called death.

Every pursuit of human endeavor has associated evil that must be eradicated. Some evil are more deeply rooted and obscure while others are obvious. You must unerringly

Designed To Fight, Destined To Win

distinguish the truth from false, the real from the unreal, the shadow from the substance, the effect from the causes and then pursue the imperishable undeviating principles of God.

There are different allurements of the world dressed in different attractive garbs. There are varying degrees of evil with same intent - destruction. If you look, you will see. The daylight is only hidden to the blind. The truth is only hidden to them who choose to be morally blinded. The secrete of the heart is revealed by opportunity and circumstance. What comes out of your mouth reveals the secrete of the heart. You must conduct an introspective soul searching, examining and rectifying your heart and motive to discover the evil in you that must be eradicated. If you look within searchingly and sincerely, you will discover and eradicate the evil therein, yielding yourself to virtuous life which is the zenith of self-mastery, with unshaken resolve to "press on to perfection". Then you will not depend on the mercy of your disposition. Then you will have good success. Success built on inward quality cannot be shaken. Success built on righteousness will endure forever.

Maintain love and live in love toward all. Manifest the fruit of the Spirit - love, joy, peace, long-suffering, kindness, goodness, faithfulness, meekness, temperance, self-control - under all circumstances and vicissitudes. Manifest the same gentle spirit toward those who oppose and attack you as toward those who agree with you.

Guided by Wisdom

Don't overly pay attention to the transient cares and affairs of this world.

You are called to live a holy life. "I BESEECH you therefore brethren, by the mercies of God, that you present your bodies a living sacrifice, holy acceptable to God, which is your reasonable service. And do not be conformed to this world: but be transformed by the renewing of your mind, that you may prove what is that good, and acceptable, and perfect, will of God" (Romans 12:1-2). "This book of the law shall not depart from your mouth; but you shall meditate in it day and night, that you may observe to do according to all that is written in it. For then you will make your way prosperous, and then you will have good success. Have I not commanded you? Be strong and of good courage; do not be afraid, nor be dismayed: for the Lord your God is with you wherever you go" (Joshua 1:8-9). You must study the Word of God and get educated on the nature of this war and the weapons needed for offensive and defensive battle against the enemy.

The most unsettling thing to do when under attack is to give up in despair and dissolution. You must not run scared of the devil, or give up in despair, weariness, or jitteriness. You must be unruffled, self-assured in your confidence in the Lord. This battle demands confidence and firmness of conviction. You must never lack calmness and firmness, which are so hard to preserve in times of war. You must be urbane, articulate, well informed, and unflinching in your faith to successfully

Designed To Fight, Destined To Win

fight this battle. Without firm resolution, no great result can be achieved. Your unwavering faith will make a declaration that will resonate and reverberate beyond the confines of your present circumstances to the spiritual world. "And the evil spirit answered and said, "'Jesus I know, and Paul I know; but who are you?'" (Acts 19:15).

(P&P)

Guided by Wisdom

MEDITATION

1. Motives determine direction.

2. Wrong motives lead to wrong moves, and wrong moves can be deadly.

3. Verification of motives can lead to sound judgment.

4. Why something is done determines what is done.

5. Why something is said determines what is said

6. What others say about you doesn't count. Only what God says or what you say about you counts.

7. When your strength depends on someone else, you will eventually become a slave to that person.

8. Wisdom requires you to put on the garment of the perfect law of God.

9. Determine to ignore and starve voices of temptation forever. Ignore them and live them unheeded, unconditionally abandoned and allowed to perish through starvation.

13

Nullify, Frustrate and Defeat the Enemy

The opportunity to nullify, frustrate and defeat the enemy is provided by the enemy himself unwittingly. The enemy will always leave a track for his own defeat. Daniel governed so well that King Darius wanted to put him in charge of Babylon. But the other officials were jealous of Daniel's success. Because of jealousy, the officials conspired to destroy Daniel. When the king's staffs conspired to destroy Daniel, they destroyed themselves in the process (see Daniel 6:24).

Nebuchadnezzar the King created a golden "god" whom all his subjects were ordered to worship. When three of God's servants refused to bow down before the golden "god," King Nebuchadnezzar was enraged and ordered them to be thrown into the fiery furnace and burned alive. When Shadrach, Meshach, and Abednego were thrown into the fiery furnace, the men who threw them into the fire were destroyed by the fire (Daniel 3:23). "Let the wicked fall into their own nets, while that I escape

Guided by Wisdom

safely" (Psalm 141:10). "The righteousness of the perfect shall direct his way: but the wicked shall fall by his own wickedness. The righteousness of the upright shall deliver them: but transgressors shall be taken in their own naughtiness" (Proverb 11:5-6, KJV). **(P&P)**

14

Make God Your Partner

They that side with God always win. If you don't want to lose in life, make God your partner. Making God your partner means making Him number one in everything you do. People who are unwilling to lose in life always win. Refuse to be intimidated by anybody, anything, anyplace, anytime. You are in an advantage position because you "waited for the city which has foundations, whose builder and maker is God" (Hebrews 11:10). "Nevertheless the solid foundation of God stands, having this seal; The Lord knows those who are His, and, Let every one who names the name of Christ depart from iniquity" (2 Timothy 2:19). "Laying up in store for themselves a good foundation against the time to come, that they may lay hold on eternal life" (1 Timothy 6:19, KJV).

15

Idols of Today = Demons of Tomorrow

The sin you allow today will destroy you tomorrow. The enemy you play with today will master you tomorrow. The idols of today will be the demons of tomorrow. "If your brother, the son of your mother, your son or your daughter, the wife of your bosom, or your friend who is as your own soul, secretly entices you, saying, 'Let us go and serve other gods,' which you have not known, neither you nor your fathers, of the gods of the people which *are* all around you, near to you or far off from you, from *one* end of the earth to the *other* end of the earth, you shall not consent to him or listen to him, nor shall your eye pity him, nor shall you spare him or conceal him" (Deuteronomy 13:6-8).

For our spiritual well-being, the old nature must be starved. This is what the apostle had in mind when he said, "Make no provision for the flesh, to *fulfill its* lusts" (Romans 13:14). To starve the old nature, to make no provision for the flesh, means that we abstain from everything that would stimulate our carnality; that we

Guided by Wisdom

avoid, as we would a plague, all that is calculated to prove injurious to our spiritual welfare. Not only must we deny ourselves the pleasures of sin and abstain from everything upon which we cannot ask God's blessing. Our affections are to be set upon things above, and not upon things upon the earth (Colossians 3:2). **(P&P)**

16

Fighting on Your Own Volition and Terms

A skillful fighter fights only on his own terms, volition, and time. David fought and defeated Goliath on his own volition with a tool of his choice: a sling and a stone, not with tools supplied by Saul. "David refused to fight Goliath with armor, helmet of brass, and coat of mail, for he said I have not tested them So David took them off '" (1 Samuel 17:39). A spiritual battle can never be won by logically thinking. "Not by might nor by power, but by My Spirit,' Says the LORD of hosts " (Zachariah 4:6).

Designed To Fight, Destined To Win

Their were three easily recognizable people in the battle during the battle between David and Goliath. They were David, Goliath, and the third man, not to mention God and the angelic hosts. Goliath was clearly outnumbered, but he did not know it. The third man is hardly ever mentioned anywhere. Before David engaged in the battle, the man who bore the shield went before him. (1 Samuel 17:41). The man went before David with a shield to protect David. In the same way, surround yourself with ever-ready prayer warriors and spiritual combat partners, without short circuiting your personal prayer responsibilities because of additional help you are getting from prayer warriors and your spiritual combat partners. Other than the prayer warriors and spiritual combat partners, God is your invincible, victorious combat partner! You can see that you are clearly in a vantage position. As a skillful fighter, here are some things to always remember:

1. Establish God's given goal.
2. Walk obediently before God in the process of pursing that goal.
3. Rely upon the Holy Spirit to practice God's given principles.
4. Maintain a resolute trust in the Lord.
5. Always fight in the name of the Lord of Host.
6. Never fight a battle in your own strength.
7. You must fight only according to God's instructions, following the direction of the Holy Spirit.
8. You must put on the whole armor of God.

Guided by Wisdom

9. Set the atmosphere for the battle. When you set the atmosphere, your faith is resolutely anchored in God's strength; then fear will resonate and reverberate in the enemy's camp.
10. Declare victory over the enemy in the name of the Lord of Hosts.
11. Let the enemy know that he is fighting against God.
12. Recognize and use your special abilities. Employ skills you have perfected, and use proven weapons.
13. Recognize that the enemy has no covenant with God, but you do.
14. In every battle, seek to make God known as the most powerful.
15. In every battle, give God the glory.
16. Reminisce on your past victories in the face of the present battle. Never cower in fear.
17. Recognize that the battle is the Lord's.
18. Remember that the Lord will deliver you from the hands of your enemy.
19. Always expect a reward. David was rewarded (1 Samuel 17). **(P&P)**

17

Resist Enticement to Battle

Never fight a battle by enticement - those who do are not wise. Be careful to whom you listen. Be careful who is enticing and arousing you to a battle; your best interest may not be on their mind. Motives determine direction. Wrong motives lead to wrong moves, and wrong moves can be deadly. Verification of motives can lead to sound judgment. Why something is done determines what is done, and why something is said determines what is said.

Never associate with an evil person or people to achieve your goal, because the evil person or people always operate with the wrong motives. Never commit completely to anyone or to any side except to God and to yourself. Never help the wicked to a battle. "Why should you help the wicked and love those who hate the Lord?" (2 Chronicle.19:2 NLT).

Jehoshaphat was enticed to join forces with Ahab, to fight a battle in which but for the mercy of God he almost lost his life. Jehoshaphat sought and received counsel from the Lord through Micah the prophet. In disobedience to

Guided by Wisdom

God, after hearing from the prophet concerning the battle, Jehoshaphat went ahead anyway to help Ahab. Ahab disguised himself to protect himself from harm, while directing Jehoshaphat into a deadly battle in royal regalia, making Jehoshaphat the logical target for attack. Jehoshaphat indeed became the target of the enemy's attack.

Be very careful because those that will entice, arouse, and send you to a battle do not mind your very destruction. Targeted for destruction in the battle, Jehoshaphat cried out to God for help, and God helped him by turning the attack away from him (2 Chronicles 18:1-34; 19:2). Jehoshaphat was a good man, but also a "man *pleaser*." Man pleasers are directly and indirectly under human control and manipulation.

Our relationship with one another must always be both horizontal and vertical – horizontal to one another but, vertical to God. The horizontal relationship must harmonize with the vertical relationship, which is the Divine order. If your horizontal and vertical relationships are not intertwined, you have a problem. Inharmonious horizontal relationship is disorder rooted in the soil of ignorance. Inharmonious relationship is disobedience and evil. All disobedience is corrective and remedial, and are therefore not permanent. Resist and refuse any inharmonious relationship. God must be pleased first before man.

To be at the mercy of your disposition is not only to be impotent, but a victim to an enervating indulgence, and

Designed To Fight, Destined To Win

on your way to destruction. Do not go out of your way and mind trying to please people. You can lose everything, including your very life, trying to please people against the will of God. Don't do anything without hearing from God. Your success and your eternal life depend on hearing from God. Follow the inward guide, the infallible voice of the Holy Spirit. Assume your rightful position in close personal relationship with God in every detail of your life. Remember, "He who is in you is greater than he who is in the world" (1 John 4:4).   **(P&P)**

Guided by Wisdom

MEDITATION

1. The sin you allow today will destroy you tomorrow.

2. The enemy you play with today will master you tomorrow.

3. The idols of today will be the demons of tomorrow.

4. A skillful fighter fights only on his own terms, volition, and time.

5. Never fight a battle by enticement - those who do are not wise.

6. There is no such thing as a penalty-free sin. The inevitable consequence of sin is penalty otherwise called death.

7. The truth is only hidden to them who choose to be morally blinded.

8. The secrete of the heart is revealed by opportunity and circumstance.

9. If you look within searchingly and sincerely, you will discover and eradicate the evil therein.

10. Manifest the same gentle spirit toward those who

Designed To Fight, Destined To Win

oppose and attack you as toward those who agree with you.

11. The most unsettling thing to do when under attack is to give up in despair and dissolution.

12 Never commit completely to anyone or to any side except to God and to yourself.

Guided by Wisdom

18

The Wicked Will be Frustrated

People with diabolical disposition have no hope of victory. He who knows he will lose has already lost, but he who is anchored in God has already won. Evil, wicked, and sinful people will ultimately meet their demise both now and eternally, if they fail to repent. "Evil shall slay the wicked: and those who hate the righteous shall be condemned" (Psalm 34:21).

Jezebel determined to destroy Elijah the man of God because of her evil disposition (1 King 19:2). When Naboth refused to give Ahab his vineyard, his father's inheritance, Jezebel conspired to kill Naboth to take the vineyard. Ahab's willing compliance with Jezebel's scheme to confiscate Naboth's vineyard made him guilty of murder and theft. And God said to Ahab, "In the place where dogs licked the blood of Naboth, dogs shall lick your blood, even yours" (1 Kings 21:19b). To Jezebel the Lord said, "The dogs shall eat Jezebel by the wall of Jezreel" (1 Kings 21:23). And the Lord said to Jehu, "You

Designed To Fight, Destined To Win

shall strike down the house of Ahab your master, that I may avenge the blood of My servants the prophets, and the blood of all the servants of the Lord, at the hand of Jezebel. For the whole house of Ahab shall perish: and I will cut off from Ahab all the males of Israel, both bond and free. So I will make the house of Ahab like the house of Jeroboam the son of Nebat, and like the house of Baasha the son of Ahijah. The dogs shall eat Jezebel on the plot of ground at Jezreel, and there shall be none to bury her" (2 Kings 9:7-10).   **(P&P)**

19

Your Enemy Will Always Lie

The enemy will use all subterfuge, from cajoling to direct threats, to insidious obstacles and pressures, to try to incriminate and destroy you. This is an antediluvian stratagem employed by the devil to blindfold you. "Be sober, be vigilant; because your adversary the devil, as a roaring lion, walks about like a roaring lion, seeking whom he may devour: Resist him, steadfast in the faith, knowing that the same sufferings are

Guided by Wisdom

experienced by your brotherhood in the world" (1 Peter 5:8-9). "He devises evil continually; he sows discord. Therefore calamity shall come suddenly; suddenly he shall be broken without remedy" (Proverbs 6:14-16). "These six things the Lord hates, Yes, seven are an abomination to him: A proud look, a lying tongue, Hands that shed innocent blood, A heart that devises wicked plans, feet that are swift in running to evil. A false witness who speaks lies and one who sows discord among brethren" (Proverbs 6:16-19). Ziba lied to David against Mephiboshet to gain favor from King David on several occasions (2 Samuel 16:1-4; 19:24-27) .

Satan is the father of lies. Truth is of God, lies are of the devil. Don't believe the lies of the devil. To the enemy the scripture said, "You are of your father the devil, and the desires of your father you want to do. He was a murderer from the beginning, and does not stand in the truth, because there is no truth in him. When he speaks a lie, he speaks of his own resources, for he is a liar and the father of it" (John 8:44). "The wicked are estranged from the womb: they go astray as soon as they are born, speaking lies" (Psalm 58:3). **(P&P)**

Designed To Fight, Destined To Win

20

The Influence of Environment

Your environment influences you consciously and subconsciously, just as you can influence your environment. But you are not your environment, and your environment is not you. You are not made by your circumstances; rather, your circumstances reveal to you who you are. It is a psychological fact that you can influence your environment and thoughts. If you do so consciously and with high purpose, you can change your habits and attitudes for the better.

Your environment can affect you positively or negatively. Your environment can make or break you if you let it get into you. You must decide what you let get into or out of you. There is a saying that, "You are a product of your environment." This is because people have a tendency to adopt the attitudes of those within their environment and those they spend time with, positively or negatively. Therefore, be environment conscious. Choose the environment that will best develop you toward your

Guided by Wisdom

objective. In a battle you must be constantly conscious of your surroundings. The influence of the people around you has a powerful effect on how you will end up in life - a success or a failure. The Word of God admonishes us to avoid the company of the ungodly. "Blessed *is* the man who walks not in the counsel of the ungodly, Nor stands in the path of sinners" (Psalm 1:1)

If you want to be successful, don't keep company with lazy and unmotivated people; rather, keep company with people of vision and motivation. It has been said that, "Nothing can stop the man with the right mental attitude from achieving his goal; nothing on earth can help the man with the wrong mental attitude." Environment can determine success or failure, just like attitude can determine success or failure. It is your choice to determine what your environment puts in you and the attitude that must come from within you. Excellent attitude towards life and a careful selection of what your environment puts in you can propel you to tremendous success.

Analyze your present environment carefully. Are the things around you helping you towards success or failure. The Spirit of God will speak to you concerning your environment. Do not dismiss God's warnings. When you dismiss God's warnings, you will set yourself up for heartache and disappointment. "Be sober, be vigilant; because your adversary the devil walks about like a roaring lion, seeking whom he may devour" (1 Peter 5:8).

Designed To Fight, Destined To Win

Change any environment, friends, associations, and goals, habits, and mannerisms that cannot develop you towards your objective. Understand that oppressors are ignorantly working for the devil. Anything that is not helping to build you up is tearing you down knowingly or unknowingly. Anything that is not changing you for the better is unnecessary in your life. Fault finders are stressed out, worrying about other peoples faults. Fault finders complain, condemn, and criticize. Wise people respect and praise others in what they do right. Wise people respect God's creation.

Dislodge the many suppressive and oppressive influences that have plagued and bombarded your life, disrupting your progress, forcing and making a mediocre person out of you. Suppressive influences are the voices that speak of your supposed inadequacies: You are too tall, too short, too white, too black, uneducated, too fat, too skinny, you can't talk, you talk too much, If it is not this, it is always something else. You must fight off these suppressive satanic influences.

The perishable opinions of other people should never define you. You must believe in yourself. If you don't believe in yourself, how can you convince others to believe in you? If you can't trust yourself, how can you convince others to trust you? Believe and trust in yourself and experience the consequent peace, success, and tranquility.

Guided by Wisdom

Do not forget the need for regular self-examination. If you judge yourself and take corrections, you will not be judged. God in His wisdom and love designed and destined you to win. You are a winner, whether you know it or not. What you say to yourself about yourself determines the fulfillment of the promise that is in you. Once God promised it, it is yours.

Your future is as bright as the promises in the Bible. Refuse to accept any false perception about yourself from yourself contrary to the promises of God. What others say about you doesn't count. Only what God says or what you say about you counts. It is written, "For by your words you will be justified, and by your words you will be condemned" (Mathew 12:37). "You are snared by the words of your mouth; you are taken by the words of your mouth." (Proverbs 6:2). "Death and life are in the power of the tongue: and those who love it will eat its fruit." (Proverbs 18:21). Living in the inside of you is the "God who gives life to the dead, and calls those things which do not exist as though they did." (Romans 4:17b). You are made in the image of that God. **(P&P)**

Designed To Fight, Destined To Win

MEDITATION

1. Silence can never be misquoted

2. Knowing when not to speak is as important as knowing when to speak.

3. Your greatest weakness can stop your greatest desire

4. Keep company with people of vision and motivation.

5. Environment can determine success or failure, just like attitude can determine success or failure.

6. Excellent attitude towards life and a careful selection of what your environment puts in you can propel you to tremendous success.

7. When you dismiss God's warnings, you will set yourself up for heartache and disappointment.

8. Anything that is not helping to build you up is tearing you down knowingly or unknowingly.

9. Anything that is not changing you for the better is unnecessary in your life.

Guided by Wisdom

21

Depend On God's Strength

A skillful fighter does not depend on his/her own strength or on the strength of others. When you depend on others for strength instead of depending on God, you are calling for more wars, more problems, and more heartaches for yourself, though it may not be noticeable, apparent or visible at first. When your strength depends on someone else, you will eventually become a slave to that person. Anyone on whose strength you depend, will eventually make you a slave. You will eventually be subservient to the petty interest of the person to whom your strength depends.

You are a person of power when you have your heart and mind fixed on God's strength. You are a person of power when you remain calm, calculated, and unmoved, trusting in the Lord while all others are swayed by some emotion or passion. If you wage this war with your own strength and power alone, you will soon be reduced to weakness and inactivity. You will soon succumb completely instead of acting with force and determination. You will

Designed To Fight, Destined To Win

encounter insurmountable difficulties, the fatigue will be too great, and the provisions impossible. Therefore depend only on God for strength and power. No struggle is too big for God. No question is unanswerable. No problem is too difficult.

The Word of God declares, "Through You we will push down our enemies; Through your name we will trample those who rise up against us. For I will not trust in my bow, nor shall my sword save me. But You have saved us from our enemies, and have put to shame those who hated us" (Psalm 44:5-7). When King Asa relied on God he was victorious, but when he relied on the king of Syria, his purpose was defeated, to which God said, "You have done foolishly; therefore from now on, you shall have wars" (2 Chronicles 16.9b). "And at that time Hanani the seer came to Asa king of Judah, and said unto him, Because you have relied on the king of Syria, and not relied on the Lord your God, therefore the army of the king of Syria escaped out of your hand. Where the Ethiopians and the Lubims not a huge army with very many chariots and horsemen? Yet because you relied on the Lord, He delivered them into your hand. For the eyes of the Lord run to and fro throughout the whole earth, to show Himself strong on behalf of those whose heart is loyal to Him'" (2 Chronicles 16:7-9). When God showed up, a slingshot from David killed Goliath. When God showed up, a rod from Moses' hand parted the Red Sea. When God showed up, one last pancake from the widow of Zarephath began her harvest. When God shows up on your behalf, who can stand against Him?   **(P&P)**

Guided by Wisdom

22

Numbers Don't Matter

Never focus on the number of your enemies. Elisha ignored the number of his enemies; he knew the Word of God (see 2 King 6:16-23). Elijah also ignored the number of his enemies. (see1 Kings18:20-40). Hezekiah king of Judah ignored the number of his enemies and their might; he knew the enemy can only fight with the arm of the flesh. Asa knew that the number of his enemies were nothing with his God. Daniel too ignored the number of his enemies. "Do not be afraid nor dismayed because of this great multitude, for the battle is not yours, but God's. … You will not need to fight in this battle. Position yourselves, stand still, and see the salvation of the Lord, who is with you" (2 Chronicles 20:15,17). The scripture declares, 'Be strong and courageous; do not be afraid nor dismayed before the king of Assyria, nor before all the multitude that *is* with him; for *there are* more with us than with him. With him *is* an arm of flesh; but with us *is* the LORD our God, to help us and to fight our battles.' And the people were strengthened by the words of Hezekiah king of Judah" (2 Chronicle 32:7,8). "And Asa cried out to the Lord his

Designed To Fight, Destined To Win

God, and said, 'Lord, it is nothing for you to help, whether with many, or with those who have no power: help us, O Lord our God, for we rest on You, and in Your name we go against this multitude. O Lord, You art our God; Do not let man prevail against You" (2 Chronicles 14:9-11).

You must put your trust in God's power, not on your outward circumstances. God works in ways you cannot even imagine. The Israelites watched God destroy Pharaoh's armies without their having to lift a finger. David defeated Goliath by the power of God, using a single smooth stone. Gideon's three hundred soldiers defeated the armies of the Midianites by the power of God. God's promise states that, "Five of you shall chase a hundred, and a hundred of you shall put ten thousand to flight; your enemies shall fall by the sword before you" (Leviticus 26:8). A similar promise states that, "One man of you shall chase a thousand, for the LORD your God *is* He who fights for you, as He promised you" (Joshua 23:10). **(P&P)**

23

Size or Status Don't Matter

Never focus on the size or status of your enemy. Don't be afraid or discouraged by the size of the task, because the infinite resources of heaven will back you up. Instead of being discouraged by the size of the task, you should be encouraged by the limitless power of God. David ignored the size of Goliath, his sword, his spear, his shield, his influence, and his power (1 Samuel 17:45-47).

God is awesome. We know that the stormy wind and the angry wave were hushed at a single word from Him. We know that a legion of demons could not resist His authoritative command. We know that He parted the Red Sea and let the children of Israel walk through on dry ground. We know that our God is clothed with omnipotence; therefore, no prayer is too hard for Him to answer, no need too great for Him to supply, no passion too strong for Him to subdue. We know that He is "the high and lofty One Who inhabits eternity, whose name is

Holy" (Isaiah 57:15). We know that "Every good gift and every perfect gift is from above, and comes down from the Father of lights, with whom there is no variation or shadow of turning" (James 1:17). **(P&P)**

24

The Power of Discernment

Discernment is a critical weapon of warfare. Discernment is an intuitive wisdom key. Discernment is knowing supernaturally without empirical knowledge. It is the ability to interpret events and to understand the true nature of the situations. It is the ability to judge a situation accurately and clearly from God's viewpoint. It is the ability to make right appraisals and godly judgment. It enables you to see behind the facades that mask the truth. It shows you the way through the maze of options that face you. Like the sun burns away the fog, discernment cuts through confusion and distractions. Whereas the devil is the "father of lies," God is the father of the truth, and He gives discernment to those who seek it. "Discernment of spirit" is a gift of the Spirit. "To another the working of miracles, to another prophecy, to another discerning of spirits, to another

Guided by Wisdom

different kinds of tongues, to another the interpretation of tongues" (1 Corinthians 12:10). Discernment guarantees the quality of choices, and prevents you from tripping over the lies and deceptions of the devil. "The fear of the Lord is the beginning of wisdom, And the knowledge of the Holy One is understanding. For by me your days will be multiplied, and years of life will be added to you" (Proverbs 9:11). "My son, let them not depart from your eyes: keep sound wisdom and discretion: So they will be life to your soul and grace to your neck. Then you will walk safely in your way, and your foot will not stumble" (Proverbs 3:21-23).

Ask God to give you discernment. Work with the Spirit of God in you. Perfect discernment is only possible from the Holy Spirit. "But God has revealed them to us through His Spirit. For the Spirit searches all things, yes, the deep things of God. ...Now we have received, not the spirit of the world, but the Spirit who is from God; that we might know the things that have been freely given to us by God. These things we also speak, not in words which man's wisdom teaches, but which the Holy Spirit teaches, comparing spiritual things with spiritual. But the natural man does not receive the things of the Spirit of God: for they are foolishness to him: nor can he know them, because they are spiritually discerned. But he who is spiritual judges all things, yet himself is rightly judged by no one. For who has known the mind of the Lord, that he may instruct Him? But we have the mind of Christ" (1 Corinthians 2:10-16). "I am your servant; give me

Designed To Fight, Destined To Win

understanding, that I may know your testimonies" (Psalm 119:125).

"Oh, how I love Your law! It *is* my meditation all the day. You, through Your commandments, make me wiser than my enemies; For they *are* ever with me. I have more understanding than all my teachers, For Your testimonies *are* my meditation. þI understand more than the ancients, Because I keep Your precepts. I have restrained my feet from every evil way, That I may keep Your word. I have not departed from Your judgments, For You Yourself have taught me. How sweet are Your words to my taste, *Sweeter* than honey to my mouth! Through Your precepts I get understanding; Therefore I hate every false way. Your word *is* a lamp to my feet and a light to my path" (Psalm 119:97-105). **(P&P)**

25

The Power of Silence

Silence can never be misquoted. Wisdom is knowing when to speak, when to be silent, and when to mind your speech. Knowing when not to speak is as important as knowing when to speak. If you must speak, be discreet. Discretion of speech is more than eloquence.

Guided by Wisdom

"The tongue of the wise is health. A wholesome tongue is a tree of life" (Proverbs 12:18; 15:4, KJV). "Do not speak in the hearing of a fool, For he will despise the wisdom of your words" (Proverbs 23:9).

Your greatest weakness can stop your greatest desire. Is your tongue your greatest weakness? What is your weakness today? Do not engage in a conversation with the enemy, but when you speak, speak the truth of the Word of God. "When wisdom enters your heart, and knowledge is pleasant to your soul; Discretion will preserve you; understanding will keep you, To deliver you from the way of evil, From the man who speaks perverse things." (Proverb. 2:10-12). "He who is void of wisdom despises his neighbor, but a man of understanding holds his peace" (Proverb 11:12). "Do not be rash with your mouth." (Ecclesiastes 5:2). "A fool's voice is known by his many words" (Ecclesiastes 5:3b). Do not let your mouth cause your flesh to sin" (Ecclesiastes 5:6). "For by your words you will be justified, and by your words you will thou be condemned" (Mathew 12:37).

Your tongue will give you away every time, if you are not living in the spirit. "Out of the abundance of the heart the mouth speaks" (Mathew 12:34b). "You are snared by the words of your mouth. You are taken by the words of your mouth. Deliver yourself like a gazelle from the hand of the hunter, And like a bird from the hand of the fowler" (Proverbs 6:2,5). In adversity, you must watch your mouth, and your thoughts. Jesus said, 'I will

Designed To Fight, Destined To Win

no longer talk much with you, for the ruler of this world is coming, and he has nothing in me' (John.14:30). "Do not answer a fool according to his folly, Lest you also be like him" (Proverbs 26:4). It is time for introspective soul searching when you catch yourself making the same mistake over and over again. Watching your mouth and thoughts are part of the battle. When you watch your thoughts, you will be able to stop your next mistake. Wrong thoughts leads to wrong decisions. Your mouth and your thoughts must always agree with the Word of God. You must not let your mouth communicate fear or unbelief to the enemy; you must not think fear or defeat; you must be confident in God and His Word. Enjoy peace, not panic; faith, not fear; commitment, not compromise. "Let it not even be named among you, as is fitting for saints; neither filthiness, nor foolish talking, nor coarse jesting, which are not fitting" (Ephesians 5:3-4). If your speech cannot be better than silence, then be at least silent. The less you speak the more costly and valuable your speech will become.

In economics, if demand is held constant, an increase in supply leads to a decreased price, while a decrease in supply leads to an increased price. An unbridled tongue has the potential of shortening your life. An unrestrained tongue can set a house on fire. "The tongue is a fire, a world of iniquity: the tongue is so set among our members that it defiles the whole body, and sets on fire the course of nature: and it is set on fire of hell. For every kind of beasts, and of birds, and of serpents, and of things in the sea, is tamed, and has been tamed by mankind: But

Guided by Wisdom

no man can tame the tongue; it is an unruly evil, full of deadly poison" (James 3:6-8.). The tongue can be a deadly poison. An unrestrained tongue is a satanic weapon of committing dual murder, first without contact and then by contact. For example, Satan can use person A's tongue to assassinate person B's character or conduct, and then turn around and use person B's gun to kill person A physically. This is a tragedy that can and should be avoided. Excessive talking leads to sin, wearies others, and distracts you from your responsibilities. Lies, destructive criticisms, gossip, and stupidity are undeniably prominent with too much talking.

Jesus remained silent when the devil approached Him. "I will no longer talk much with you, for the ruler of this world is coming, and he has nothing in Me." (John.14:30). Talk well of your friends, and of your enemies be silent. Remember silence can never be misquoted. "Speak evil of no one" (Titus 3:2). "Sound speech that cannot be condemned, that one who is an opponent may be ashamed, having nothing evil to say of you" (Titus 2:8). **(P&P)**

26

Nothing Is Constant

Do not look at any situation as it first appears because nothing is constant. Nothing is as bad as it first appears. Everything changes. Nothing remains without change. The only thing that does not change is change itself. The ignorance of this law results in periods of unreasoning enthusiasm on the one hand, and depression on the other. Man then becomes the victim of the tide when he should be its master. When battles come to the worst, they generally mend. It is only when you see it from your eyes that you feel defeated. See it from God's eyes, and you have already won. If you can see the invisible, you can do the impossible.

The point is that you must not lose your joy on your present circumstances. Warfare always precedes blessings. Battles are gateways to promotion. Battles can either challenge or threaten you. Fight the battle deterministically. Your beliefs, when anchored in God, paves your way to victory. Elisha and his servant saw a supernatural picture of support from heaven quite different from what the physical eyes revealed. When

Guided by Wisdom

David faced Goliath, he did not consider defeat; he expected victory in the name of the Lord. David and Joseph respectively anchored their beliefs in God, and received their promotion and the gift of victory. (see Genesis 39-41; 1 Samuel17, 2; Samuel 2). "Do not fear: for those who are with us are more than those who are with them. And Elisha prayed, and said, Lord, I pray, open his eyes, that he may see. Then the Lord opened the eyes of the young man, and he saw. And behold, the mountain was full of horses and chariots of fire round about Elisha" (2 Kings 6:16-17). **(P&P)**

Designed To Fight, Destined To Win

MEDITATION

1. Anyone on whose strength you depend, will eventually make you a slave.

2. If you wage this war with your own strength and power alone, you will soon be reduced to weakness and inactivity.

3. Never focus on the number of your enemies

4. Never focus on the size or status of your enemy.

5. Discernment is a critical weapon of warfare.

6. Silence can never be misquoted.

7. Knowing when not to speak is as important as knowing when to speak.

8. Your greatest weakness can stop your greatest desire.

9. Nothing is as bad as it first appears.

10. Warfare always precedes blessings.

11. Battles are gateways to promotion.

Guided by Wisdom

27

Live and Work by Faith

Stay focused, work by faith not by sight, feelings or present condition. Never focus on distraction. Whatever you focus on expands. If you focus on distraction, it will soon become your main attraction. Distraction is the enemy of direction. Nothing should focus your mind to fight more than the ceaseless attack from the adversary the devil, who wants to wipe you off the map into hell. This battle is fought and won only by faith. "But without faith it is impossible to please Him, for he who comes to God must believe that He is, and that He is a rewarder of those who diligently seek him" (Hebrews 11:6) "Because the foolishness of God is wiser than men, and the weakness of God is stronger than men" (1 Corinthians 1: 25).

Never believe your conscience, your senses or your feelings more than the Word of God, which is settled in heaven. We walk by faith, not by conscience, senses, or feelings. Always act according to the Word of God. Never trust in the witness of the senses or concentrate on the sense knowledge evidence whenever it violates the word

Designed To Fight, Destined To Win

of God. It is written, "Let the weak say, I am strong" (Joel 3:10). In other words, confess strength in your position of weakness. Say "I am strong" though you may feel weak at the moment, because the Lord is your strength. Your strength does not depend on you, but on the Lord. JEHOVA is your strength. (see Joel.3:10).

The weakest saint anchored in God is a dynamic force to contend with, because to fight the saint, you must first fight God. The weak child of God has one weapon - the power of God. With God, all things are possible. This battle requires a complete faith in the God who has chosen the foolish things of the world to confound the wise, and the weak things of the world to confound the things which are mighty; the God who has chosen the base things of the world and the things that are despised; the God who has chosen the things that are not to nullify the things that are, so that no one may boast before Him (see 1 Corinthians 27-29). The Word of God declares, "For we walk by faith, not by sight" (2 corinthians 5:7).

By faith Noah built an ark to save his family. By faith Abraham traveled to a foreign country, and Isaac and Jacob became heirs with him of the same promise. By faith Abraham and Sarah conceived a child when they were past age. By faith the Israelites under the leadership of Moses passed through the Red Sea as on dry land (Hebrews 11:1-39). The successful man is the average man, focused. Be determined to win. Don't be double minded. "A double minded man is unstable in all his ways" (James 1:8, KJV). Consider the race that is set

108

Guided by Wisdom

before you. Set aside every hindrance and sin which easily entangles, and run with perseverance and patience. Determine to get to the finish line, dedicating yourself to its attainment with unswerving singleness of purpose, and with the trenchant zeal of Paul the Apostle. "Press toward the mark for the prize of the high calling of God in Christ Jesus" (Philippians 3:14). **(P&P)**

28

Focus on Doing Right

Don't let anyone distract your focus. Wisdom is the power to put your time and knowledge to the proper use. Wisdom is the power to make the right decision every time. Wisdom is the power to make righteous decision every time. Always make decisions that will please God, and reject decisions that will not please Him. Make decision based on moral principle. No matter how much pressure there is, never allow others to force you into making immoral and unethical decisions. Never break moral principle to bow to others opinions. Do what is right, even if it's unpopular. Do right when it seems better to do wrong. The secret of failure is trying to

Designed To Fight, Destined To Win

please everybody. Being preoccupied with doing good instead of doing right is wrong. Good things are what people want you to do. The right things are what you should always do. You don't need to be too radical in defending yourself when you are doing the right thing. Right is its own defense. Always do the right thing. This will gratify some people and generate hatred in others. True happiness comes from doing what's right, not just what makes you feel good. The devil's weapon is to get you distracted by doing good things instead of right things.

Uzza was a good man doing what he thought was a good thing. He died in the process of doing a good thing, and not the right thing. "So they carried the ark of God on a new cart from the house of Abinadab, and Uzza and Ahio drove the cart. ...When they came to Chidon's, threshing floor, Uzza put out his hand to hold the ark, for the oxen stumbled. Then the anger of the Lord was aroused against Uzza, and He struck him because he put his hand to the ark: and he died there before God." (1 chronicles 13:7,10). **Good men and women die doing good things**. Uzza was not a Levite. "No one may carry the ark of God but the Levites, for the Lord has chosen them to carry the ark of God, and to minister before Him for ever" (1 Chronicles 15:2).

You were not created to do everything. You were not created to meet every need. You were not created to solve every problem. You were created to solve *some* problems on this earth. The problem you were created to

Guided by Wisdom

solve is your assignment. You must not let anyone distract you from your assignment. There will always be people who will insist on taking you "out of yourself" for their own selfish agenda; resist them and refuse their offer. **Those who do not respect your assignment disqualify themselves from your relationship.** Those who criticize your assignment disqualify themselves from your attention. Those who cannot sense your integrity disqualified themselves from your relationship. **Those unwilling to discern your integrity are incapable of loyalty.**

Noah built the ark in the face of misguided criticisms. When the flood came the critics were destroyed, but Noah and his family were saved. You must ignore the opinions and offenses of people who hurt you. You must ignore false accusations of others, and you must ignore your own mistakes. When you refuse to allow the degrading comments of others to discourage you, when you remove yourself from their influence if your vision becomes threatened and you cling to God's commandment and directions, you can unleash the totality of God's power within you.

Jesus demonstrated the importance of disregarding the opinions of others. "But Jesus did not commit himself to them, because he knew all men, And had no need that anyone should testify of man: for he knew what was in man" (John 2:24-25). Always remember that:
- Those who feed your greed are dangerous.
- Those who feed your doubt are dangerous.

Designed To Fight, Destined To Win

♦ Those who feed your fear are dangerous.
♦ Those who feed your rebellion are dangerous.
♦ Anyone who justifies your sin is dangerous.
♦ Anyone who sins with you will eventually sin against you.
♦ Anyone who lies for you will eventually lie against you.
♦ Anyone who breaks the confidence of someone to you will eventually break your confidence to someone else.
♦ Anyone who gossips to you will eventually gossip against you.
♦ Anyone who trivializes your assignment is dangerous.
♦ Anyone who assault your character openly or in disguise is dangerous.
♦ Anyone who refuses to defend you in your absence is dangerous.
♦ Anyone who does not allow you to say what God said is dangerous. Say what God said anyway. "Preach the word; Be ready in season, and out of season, Convince, rebuke, exhort with all longsuffering and teaching" (2 Timothy 4:2). Neither wicked men nor devils can hinder the work of God, or shut out His presence from His people.
♦ Anyone who consistently negates any positive ideas, goals, or dreams of yours is dangerous. Negators specialize in poisoning and sabotaging positive progress of others. They unwittingly make a mediocre person out of you if you let them. Flush their opinions and advice out of your system.   **(P&P**

Guided by Wisdom

29

Victory Is a Gift

Victory is a gift, but the will to conquer is the first condition of victory. The secret of victory lies in your hearing from God and obeying God. The word of God declares, "But thanks be to God, who gives us the victory through our Lord Jesus Christ (1 Corinthians 15:57). The battle has been won before the fight started. God gave Gideon the gift of victory. "And the Lord said to him, 'Surely I will be with you, and you shall defeat the Midianites as one man' (Judges 6:16).

God gave Joshua the gift of victory. "And the Lord said to Joshua, See, I have given Jericho into your hand, its king, and the mighty men of valor" (Joshua 6:2). God gave King Asa the gift of victory. "So the Lord struck the Ethiopians before Asa, and Judah, and the Ethiopians fled." (2 Chronicles 14:12). God gave Hezekiah the gift of victory. "The Lord saved Hezekiah and the inhabitants of Jerusalem from the hand of Sennacherib the king of Assyria, and from the hand of all other, and guided them on every side" (2 Chronicles 32:22). **(P&P)**

30

Counterfeit Victory

The enemy is a master counterfeiter. He is a fake and a sham. Don't believe him. He is a defeated foe. "Then the Lord spoke to Moses and Aaron, saying, 'When Pharaoh speaks to you, saying, 'Show a miracle for yourselves," then you shall say to Aaron, "Take your rod and cast *it* before Pharaoh, *and* let it become a serpent. '" So Moses and Aaron went in to Pharaoh, and they did so, just as the Lord commanded. And Aaron cast down his rod before Pharaoh and before his servants, and it became a serpent. But Pharaoh also called the wise men and the sorcerers; so the magicians of Egypt, they also did in like manner with their enchantments. For every man threw down his rod, and they became serpents. But Aaron's rod swallowed up their rods." (Exodus 7:8-12). "But thanks be to God, who gives us the victory through our Lord Jesus Christ" (1 Corinthians 15:57). "O sing to the Lord a new song! for He has done marvelous things: His right hand, and His holy arm, have gained Him the victory" (Psalm 98:1). **(P&P)**

Guided by Wisdom

31

Your Thought Life

Never allow the enemy to reset, rewire or reconfigure your psychogenic barometer. As a man thinks, so is he. "As he thinks in his heart, so is he" (Proverbs 23:7). "Keep your heart with all diligence, For out of it spring the issues of life" (Proverbs 4:23). In other words, protect and guard your heart with all diligence. Your thoughts determine your character. You must train yourself to master all the critical gates through which the enemy can take control of your life. You must post a guard constantly and with all diligence at the gates of your thoughts to reject and refuse anything that is unrighteous, ungodly, and does not conform to the Word of God for your life. The gates to master are the gates to the thoughts of your heart, namely: your ear gate, your eye gate, your mouth or tongue gate, your nose gate, and your hand gate. King David prayed to God and said, "Set a guard, O LORD, over my mouth; Keep watch over the door of my lips" (Psalm 141:3). Be very careful of what you hear, what you see, what you touch, what you taste or say, and what you smell. Whatever enters one of the gates to your heart can determines what resides in the thoughts of your

Designed To Fight, Destined To Win

heart. What resides in the thoughts of your heart determines who you are. "Apply your heart to instruction, and your ears to words of knowledge" (Proverbs 23:12). Never let your heart drift away from the living Word of God. Capture your thoughts and bring them in line with the Word of God. In complete equipoise, you must maintain absolute responsibility of guarding the state of your thoughts. Your success depends directly and indirectly on the state of your thoughts.

The enemy will always use someone to bring an evil word against you to contaminate your faith. If the enemy brings an evil report or word a trillion times, reject it a trillion times. The devil will always place people in strategic places to repeat the exact venom against you, whatever it may be, hoping that by constantly bombarding you with the venom, you will succumb. You must constantly reject the enemy's venom. The devil always want you to hear what they said about you because that is how his venom will get into you. If you waste your time thinking of his venom, you will begin to doubt yourself and the power within you. Therefore refuse to think about his venom. Do not worry about the murmurings, complaint, and suggestions of men meant for evil against you. Never agree with any negative words spoken over you by the enemy.

Thought linked with purpose is the road to accomplishment. Regardless of what your present environment may be, you will rise or fall depending on your belief system, your state of thoughts, your vision,

Guided by Wisdom

and your ideal. You must sacrifice whatever it takes to set your thoughts above your carnal indulgences. There is no success without sacrifice. For example, education may be very costly to obtain, but ignorance will cost a whole lot more. There can be no achievement without sacrifice. To achieve little, you only need to sacrifice little. To achieve much, you must sacrifice much. Be in control of your thought life. Your thoughts have power; your thoughts are energy. You can make or break your world by the way you think. Embrace strong, pure, and happy thoughts, but resist and reject thoughts of fear, doubt, malice, jealousy, envy, lust, hatred, anger, pride, rebellion, bitterness, unbelief, covetousness, cynicism, fear, disappointment, and despondency.

You must consistently live your life responsibly and righteously. Your thought is a seed. Every seed sown produces its own kind. Good thoughts bear good fruits, and bad thoughts bear bad fruits. Sow a thought, reap an act. Sow an act, reap a habit. Sow a habit, reap your character. Sow your character, reap your destiny. By controlling your thought, you can control your life within the degrees of freedom preset by the sovereign will of God. Within and outside the degrees of freedom preset for your life, God said, "For I know the thoughts that I think toward you, saith the Lord, thought of peace, and not of evil, to give you an expected end" (Jeremiah 29:11, KJV). How's your thought life? What are you putting inside your brain and heart? Your thoughts can lead to your spiritual destruction which happens subtly if you are not watchful. What enters you determines what exits you.

Designed To Fight, Destined To Win

"Do not be deceived; God is not mocked; for whatsoever a man sows, that he will also reap. For he who sows to his flesh will of the flesh reap corruption, but he who sows to the Spirit will of the Spirit reap everlasting life" (Galatians.6:7-8).

Proverbs 5 tells the story of a moral failure. A father warned his son to avoid the seductive woman. "Stay away from her," the father insists. "You will lose your self-respect and end up in debt." The father encouraged him to remain faithful to his wife and say no to all other women. But the son thought that an affair might not be so bad. His marriage had become a little boring, he reasoned. She's a nice lady. I'll just stop by and say hello. As soon as he enters her home, disaster strikes! He might as well have died. This son ignored the warning from his wise father. His actions cost him his marriage, his fellowship with God, and his reputation. His character is now trashed. His world is destroyed.

Giving in to sexual sin always takes place first in the mind. It is critical to keep lustful thoughts away from your mind. What encourages you to enjoy any kind of thought that is against the character of God? Certain friends, magazines, books, movies, or T.V. shows? Stay away from those satanic influences. Stay away from any influences that cause you to enjoy sin. Through the power of God, reject the present lustful thoughts and desires in order to protect what you love. Dedicate your thought life to God so that the character you develop will please Him. "Keep your heart with all diligence; for out of it springs the issues of life " (Proverbs 4:23). "Finally,

118

Guided by Wisdom

brethren, whatsoever things are true, whatsoever things are noble, whatsoever things are just, whatsoever things are pure, whatsoever things are lovely, whatsoever thing of good report; if there is any virtue, and if there is anything praiseworthy, meditate on these things. The things which you learned, and received and heard and saw in me, do, and the God of peace will be with you" (Philippians 4:8-9).

Your heart contains your belief system where you deposit all the seed you need. Whatever you sow, that you must reap. Take a picture of your heart. If you lack anything, check your belief system, check the seed you planted in your thought, check the state of your thoughts, check your visions, and ideals and then make the necessary changes. **Your life moves in the direction of your most dominating thought. Your mind is as strong as your weakest thought. The quality of your thoughts determine the quality of your life.** **(P&P)**

32

Seek God Before Going to Battle

Is God on your side? Is He number one in every detail of your life? Is He involved in every decision you make. If God is involved in every detail of your life, you have already won! God is an invincible, victorious combat partner! Speak the desired outcome of the battle, and God will back you up. Always speak the end result. Speak the outcome of your life, and you will get it. You will get what you want in life when you start speaking. Joshua secured victory against Jericho before he went to the battlefield because God was on his side. Joshua spoke the victory, and God confirmed the victory. "And Joshua said to the people, 'Sanctify yourselves, for tomorrow the Lord will do wonders among you'. …And the Lord said unto Joshua, 'This day I will begin to exalt you in the sight of all Israel, that they may know that, as I was with Moses, so I will be with you' (Joshua 3:5,7). "And the Lord said to Joshua, 'See, I have given Jericho into your hand, its king, and the mighty men of valor" (Joshua 6:2).

Guided by Wisdom

Gideon secured victory against the Midianites before he went to the battlefield. "And the Lord said to him, 'Surely I will be with you, and you shall defeat the Midianites as one man' (Judges 6:16).

On the other hand, Saul, after inquiring from the woman with the familiar spirit at Endor, went to war seeking for victory, but died in the battlefield. "So Saul, his three sons, and his armor bearer, and all his men died together that same day" (1 Samuel 31:6).   **(P&P)**

33

Made in the Image of God

God does not lose any battle. You are the copy of the original. God is the original, and you are an express copy of the original. For God to create man in His own image and likeness, He must have within Himself a description of Himself – characteristics, attributes, image, etc. "And God said, 'Let us make man in our image, according to Our likeness; let them have dominion over the fish of the sea, over the birds of the air, and over the cattle, over all the earth, and over every creeping thing that creeps on the earth' (Genesis 1:26).

Designed To Fight, Destined To Win

God poured out Himself into you. If you make a photocopy of any document, the copy should read exactly as the original. If you have a glass of water and pour out a portion of that water into another glass, the content of the second glass will be exactly the same chemical content ($H2O$) as that from which it is poured. It will not be orange juice just because you transferred a portion of it into another cup. The original does not lose battles; therefore, the copies will not lose battles.

Every human being is created in the image of God but everybody is not in the likeness of God. To be in the likeness of God, you must have God in you. If you are born again, as the scripture says, then you are in the likeness of God. You have God's attributes in you. When God created man in His own image and likeness, He deposited in man His own very characteristics and attributes. The more you look like your father God, the more your authority will reverberate in the kingdom of darkness. Anybody that sees you should be able to recognize who your father is. When you are in the likeness of your father, even the devil will recognize that you are of your father God. The only thing that prevents you from looking like your father God is sin, which deforms your likeness. "Your iniquities have separated you from your God" (Isaiah 59:2).

Your authority depends on maintaining the requirements of the position that you occupy as a child of God. These requirements are righteousness and holiness. Righteousness is a gift of right standing with God.

Guided by Wisdom

Holiness is living your daily life according to God's will based on your position of righteousness.   **(P&P)**

34

Avoid Your Enemy

Wisdom will guide you on when to engage in a battle and when not to engage in a battle.
There are times you need to avoid your enemy. You are not retreating, but advancing in style in another direction. "Do not enter the path of the wicked, And do not walk in the way of evil. Avoid it, do not travel on it; Turn away from it and pass on. For they do not sleep unless they have done evil; And their sleep is taken away unless they make *someone* fall. For they eat the bread of wickedness, And drink the wine of violence" (Proverbs 4:14-17). When Saul determined to kill David, David avoided Saul. "Then David fled from Naioth in Ramah, and went and said to Jonathan, 'What have I done? What is mine iniquity? And what is my sin before your father, that he seeks my life' (1 Samuel 20:1). When the Jews took counsel to kill Paul, "The disciples took him by night and let him down through the wall in a large basket"

123

Designed To Fight, Destined To Win

(Acts 9:23-25). When the Nazarenes became furious and wanted to throw Jesus off the cliff, Jesus walked right by them and went his way. (see Luke 4:14-30).

It does not matter whether strategy or valor defeats the enemy. The important thing is that the enemy is defeated and you received the gift of victory. Evil can never be satisfied. Evil can never tell the truth unless it is to its advantage. Evil left unchecked spreads like a wildfire and is very cancerous. You can never please your enemy, no matter how hard you try. Your enemy will always be antagonistic, harmful, and deadly. You can't do anything to turn a true friend off, and you can't do anything good to turn an enemy on. You can't do anything right to please an enemy. Therefore, quit trying to please your enemy. The only thing you can do to please your enemy is to die. The only time your enemy will say something good about you is when you're dead. Therefore, if you really want to go out of your way to please your enemies you must die. To live a rich life full of experiences or to live to please your enemy is a choice. Choose wisely!

(P&P)

Guided by Wisdom

MEDITATION

1. Never focus on distraction.

2. Whatever you focus on expands.

3. The weakest saint anchored in God is a dynamic force to contend with, because to fight the saint, you must first fight God.

4. The successful man is the average man, focused. A double minded man is unstable in all his ways" (James 1:8, KJV).

5. Never break moral principle to bow to others opinions.

6. The secret of failure is trying to please everybody.

7. Those unwilling to discern your integrity are incapable of loyalty.

8. Those who do not respect your assignment disqualify themselves from your relationship.

9. You were not created to do everything. You were not created to meet every need. You were not created to solve every problem.

10. Victory is a gift, but the will to conquer is the first

Designed To Fight, Destined To Win

condition of victory.

11. Never allow the enemy to reset, rewire or reconfigure your psychogenic barometer. As a man thinks, so is he. "As he thinks in his heart, so is he" (Proverbs 23:7).

12. Thought linked with purpose is the road to accomplishment.

13. There can be no achievement without sacrifice. To achieve little, you only need to sacrifice little. To achieve much, you must sacrifice much.

14. Your life moves in the direction of your most dominating thought.

15. Your mind is as strong as your weakest thought.

16. The quality of your thoughts determine the quality of your life.

17. There are times you need to avoid your enemy. You are not retreating, but advancing in style in another direction.

18. Evil can never tell the truth unless it is to its advantage.

19. Evil left unchecked spreads like a wildfire and is very cancerous.

Guided by Wisdom

20. The only time your enemy will say something good about you is when you're dead.

21. It does not matter whether strategy or valor defeats the enemy.

22. The more you look like your father God, the more your authority will reverberate in the kingdom of darkness.

23. Your authority depends on maintaining the requirements of the position that you occupy as a child of God.

24. What enters you determines what exits you.

25. Never agree with any negative words spoken over you by the enemy.

Designed To Fight, Destined To Win

35

False Prophets

The devil uses false profits, I mean false prophets, the servants of money to deceive and attack the flock of Christ. These are smooth operators, Satan's instruments of spiritual oppression, bondage, and vileness, building their own personal kingdoms with reprobate intentions. They use a combination of manipulation, scare tactics, outright threat and appeal of your God loving nature to put pressure on you to empty your bank account. They are the www.false-profit-generals-of-corruption.com. Beware and stay away from them, even the worldling, dwarfed in biblical intelligentsia and revelation have the acumen to stay away from the atrocities disconnected from the faith. One of the major impediments of living a godly life is false guides - those who under the pretence of giving divine directions, fatally deceiving and alluring people with "itching ears" into the broad road that leads to destruction. While they proffer and promise you peace and life, death and traps are on their mind unabashedly. Do not be deceived by oratorical skills devoid of righteous living. "Beware of false prophets, who come to you in sheep's clothing, but inwardly they

Guided by Wisdom

are ravenous wolves" (Mathew 7:15). They parade themselves with less than stellar quality godly life, with guaranteed ambivalence in their behavior. Their desire wittingly or unwittingly is to exsanquinate the very life out of you.

These are chocolate-talking, sweet-talking, smooth-talking politicians, prophesying to the people "smooth things," deceits, inventing easy ways to heaven, pandering to corrupt nature. They are the agents of the devil and more satanic than Satan, yet claim to be the servants of the Holy God. They are demonic agents, manipulating and controlling the people. Never let yourself be manipulated or controlled by these demonic agents. Resist anyone who would attempt to control or change your God given assignment and goals through false prophesies. "The gifts and the calling of God are irrevocable" (Romans 11:29). They are not hearing from God. They give false words, revelations, visions, dreams, and twisted half truth. They are deceitful workers. They are motivated by "love of money" not "love of souls". The end of their conversation is money. They are extortionists. Be vigilant! They promise freedom but meant intolerable burden and bondage, they promise light but meant darkness, they promise peace but meant war.

They conceive and utter from their heart words of falsehood, lips full of lies. They hurry to shed innocent blood. They are *whited* sepulchers which appear beautiful outward, but are within full of dead men's bones, hypocrisy and iniquity. "Now the Spirit expressly says, that in the latter times some will depart from the faith,

Designed To Fight, Destined To Win

giving heed to deceiving spirits and doctrines of demons, Speaking lies in hypocrisy, having their own conscience seared with a hot iron" (1 Timothy 4:1-2). "For many walk, of whom I have told you often, and now tell you even weeping, that they are the enemies of the cross of Christ: Whose end is destruction, whose God is their belly, and whose glory is in their shame, who set their mind on earthly things" (Philippians 3:18-19). "Now I urge you, brethren note those who cause divisions and offenses, contrary to the doctrine which you learned, and avoid them. For those who are such do not serve our Lord Jesus Christ, but their own belly, and by smooth words and flattering speech deceive the heart of the simple" (Romans 16:17-18). "For such are false apostles, deceitful workers, transforming themselves into apostles of Christ. And no wonder! For Satan himself transforms himself into an angel of light. Therefore it is no great thing if his ministers also transform themselves into ministers of righteousness, whose end will be according to their works" (2Corinthians 11:13-15).

There is a warning in scripture against false teachers: "There were also false prophets among the people, even as there will be false teachers among you, who will secretly bring in destructive heresies, even denying the Lord who bought them, and bring on themselves swift destruction. And many will follow their destructive ways, because of whom the way of truth will be blasphemed. By covetousness they will exploit you with deceptive words; for a long time their judgment has not been idle, and their destruction does not slumber" (2 Peter 2:1-3).

Guided by Wisdom

The Apostle Paul wrote to Timothy saying, "For the time will come when they will not endure sound doctrine; but according to their own desire, because they have itching ears, they will heap to themselves teachers, and they will turn their ears away from the truth, and be turned to fables" (2 Timothy 4:3-4). This "turning away is evidenced on every hand, therefore beware". John the Apostle gave a warning, "Do not believe every spirit, but test the spirit whether they are of God: because many false prophets have gone out into the world" (1 John 4:1). You must be on your guard against false teachers and heretical preachers. You must labor diligently to become thoroughly acquainted with God's Word for yourself, or how should you be fitted to detect these destructive seducers of souls? "Study to show thyself approved unto God, a workman that needed not be ashamed, rightly dividing the word of truth" (2 Timothy 2:15, KJV).

The genuine servants of God give evidence to their commission by the doctrine they proclaim. Their preaching is in full accord with the Word of God. Their daily walk is an example of practical godliness. Paul said, "Imitate me, just as I also imitate Christ" (1 Corinthians.11:1). You must therefore study the Word of God for yourself. "Study to show thyself approved unto God, a workman that needed not to be ashamed, rightly dividing the word of truth" (2 Timothy 2:15, KJV). "That we should no longer be children, tossed to and fro and carried about with every wind of doctrine, by the trickery of men, in the cunning craftiness of deceitful

Designed To Fight, Destined To Win

plotting, but, speaking the truth in love, may grow up in all things into Him who is the head—Christ— from whom the whole body, joined and knit together by what every joint supplies, according to the effective working by which every part does its share, causes growth of the body for the edifying of itself in love" (Ephesians 4:14-16). **(P&P)**

36

Talk the Solution

Don't talk the problem, talk the solution. Prophesy your expected victory. God said to Ezekiel, "Prophesy to these bones, and say to them, 'O dry bones, hear the word of the Lord," (Ezekiel 37:4). 'As I live,' says the Lord, 'just as you have spoken in My hearing, so I will do to you' (Numbers 28:14). "You will also declare a thing, And it will be established for you; So light will shine on your ways. When they cast *you* down, and you say, 'Exaltation *will come!*' Then He will save the humble *person.*" (Job.22:28-29).

Shadrach, Meshack, and Abednego said, "If that is the case, our God whom we serve is able to deliver us from

Guided by Wisdom

the burning fiery furnace, and He will deliver us from your hand, O king" (Daniel 3:17). "Death and life are in the power of the tongue, and those who love it will eat its fruit" (Proverbs 18:21). "For by your words you will be justified, and by your words you will be condemned" (Matthew 12:37). Your victory will start with your mouth. Speak the desired result. Let every thought and desire affirm that you already have what you asked. "Therefore I say to you, Whatever things you ask when you pray, believe that you receive them, and you will have them" (Mark 11:24). **(P&P)**

37

The Power of Agreement

Never underestimate the power of agreement. You need prayer partners. Two are better than one. Your prayer partner can be your wife, your husband, or your trusted friend who is deeply anchored in God. You shall know them by their fruits. Remember, isolation is the first step to devastation. "If two of you agree on earth as concerning anything that they ask, it will be done for them by my Father in heaven" (Matthew 18:19). Prayer

Designed To Fight, Destined To Win

partners should always pray for protection, provision, direction, wisdom, and strength. Surround yourself with ever ready prayer warriors and spiritual combat partners. They are your back-up troops. With them at your disposal you can always turn the tide of the battle.

The prayer warriors present obstacle to the enemy's approach. The prayer warriors and your spiritual combat partners are additional aid to your being constantly under prayer covering, defensively and offensively. The prayer warrior as an obstacle to the enemy serves chiefly to support your flank and to strengthen your front.

You must never short circuit your personal prayer responsibilities because of additional help you are getting from prayer warriors and your spiritual combat partners. You must intercede for others while they intercede for you. Pray persistently. Ask and keep on asking, seek and keep on seeking, knock and keep on knocking until your prayers are answered. "Because of his persistence he will rise and give him as many as he needs. So I say to you, ask, and it will be given to you; seek, and you will find; knock, and it will be opened to you" (Luke 5:8-9).

(P&P)

Guided by Wisdom

38

Don't Quit!

You might have occasional bruises, but that is expected in a war. It does not matter how you started; all that matters is how you finish. It is much better to lose a battle and win the war than to win a battle and lose the war. The man who wins may have been counted out several times, but he didn't hear the referee. Defeat never comes to any man until he admits it. One of the marks of a winner is the ability to come back in an apparent defeat. Great champions have all come back from an apparent defeat. All men fall, but great men get back up again. "For a righteous man may fall seven times and rise again: but the wicked shall fall by calamity" (Proverbs 24:16).

When the devil thought he had defeated Jesus, Jesus rose from the dead, "Having disarmed principalities and powers, He made a public spectacle of them, triumphing over them in it" (Colossians 2:15). Jesus said, "All authority has been given to Me in heaven and on earth. Go therefore and make disciples of all the nations, baptizing them in the name of the Father and of the Son

Designed To Fight, Destined To Win

and of the Holy Spirit, teaching them to observe all things that I have commanded you; and lo, I am with you always, even to the end of the world" (Matthew 28:18-20). **(P&P)**

39

If You Can Be Bought Satan Can Meet Any Price

If you can be bought, Satan can meet any price. Satan is a powerful arm-twisting bully. Do not compromise your stand with God. Satan is wise; he tempts by making rich instead of poor. He buys your soul, the very you, at any cost. He exchanges your soul for his money; with your soul in his pocket, you become miserably poor. "For the love of money is the root of all kinds of evil, for which some have strayed from the faith in their greediness, and pierced themselves through with many sorrows.. But you, O man of God, flee these things and pursue righteousness, godliness, faith, love patience, meekness." (1 Timothy 6:10-11). Every child of God will face times of testing when he/she will be ordered to bow to ungodliness. There is always a crossroad of faith when

Guided by Wisdom

you must take a stand even at the cost of your life or the risk of great personal loss. What will you do?

Shadrach, Meshach, and Abed-Nego faced such a time. They were given one simple choice: bow or die. There were no bargainings or compromises. They were ordered to bow to the golden "god" or be reduced to ashes. They chose to die instead of bowing down to an idle.

Everybody must undergo the test of responsibility. There are three tests that are common to all mankind. "For all that is in the world, the lust of the flesh, the lust of the eyes, and the pride of life, is not of the Father, but is of the world" (1 John 2:16). To develop integrity, self-discipline, and maturity, you must pass all the tests. Depend on God to master and pass the tests in these three areas of your life;

- ♦ Lust of the flesh. This is the test for physical pleasure, gratification, or appetite: food, drink, and sex
- ♦ Lust of the eyes. This is the lust of everything the eye can see. It is the test for greed and power.
- ♦ Pride of life. This is the test for motive, fame, and pride, the boasting in one's own resources and earthly things.

These tests are very important because people who cannot control their flesh are dangerous and can't be trusted. People who cannot control their greed are dangerous and can create havoc. People who do not understand power abuse it and are very dangerous. Power without wisdom are like a heavy ax without an edge.

Designed To Fight, Destined To Win

**Whatever you are free from you are qualified for.
Whatever you abuse will eventually destroy you.**
Whatever you are free from you can be trusted with.
Whatever you are free from cannot control you. When
you are free from the need for power, you are qualified
for authority. **Whatever you compromise to gain, you
will eventually lose.** Be careful what you are
compromising. Be aware that temptation must come, and
it is a fact of life. Nobody has any immunity against
temptation. Be aware that:

- Temptation can come to any person.
- Temptation can come at any period.
- Temptation can come at any place.
- Temptation can come at any point.

"Therefore let him who thinks he stands take heed lest he
fall. No temptation has overtaken you except such as is
common to man; but God is faithful, who will not allow
you to be tempted beyond what you are able, but with
the temptation will also make the way of escape, that you
may be able to bear it" (1 Corinthians 10:12-13).

Jesus passed all three tests, and was then ministered to by
the angels. "Angels came and ministered to Him"
(Mathew 4:11). When was the last time you recognized
that the angels ministered to you? Do you even know or
recognize that there are angels all around you? Pass the
tests today and the angels will minister to you, to your
recognition. To overcome temptations, do what Jesus did.

1.   You have to be a son or daughter of God. Jesus

Guided by Wisdom

was declared the Son of God. "And the Holy Spirit descended in a bodily form like a dove upon him, and a voice came from heaven, which said, You art My beloved Son; in You I am well pleased" (Luke 3:22). To be the son or daughter of God, you must receive Jesus and be born again. "But as many as received Him, to them He gave the right to become children of God, to those who believe in His name: Who were born, not of blood, nor of the will of the flesh, nor of the will of man, but of God" (John 1:12-13).

2.   You have to be full of the Holy Ghost. Jesus was full of the Holy Ghost. "Then Jesus being filled with the Holy Spirit, returned from Jordan, and was led by the Spirit into the wilderness" (Luke 4:1).

3.   You have to live by the Word of God, and be satisfied with who you are and what you have. Jesus mastered the Word of God. He knew who He was and was self-contained. "But Jesus answered him, saying, 'It is written, Man shall not live by bread alone, but by every word of God' (Luke 4:4).

4.   You have to reject false gods. Never seek for easy shortcuts, instant fame, or sudden success if the Word of God is violated. Jesus rejected false gods, never worshiped any false god, and never took any shortcut to instance fame. "And Jesus

Designed To Fight, Destined To Win

answered and said to him, 'Get thee behind me, Satan! For it is written, "You shall worship the Lord your God, and him only you shall serve"' (Luke.4:8).

5. You must never tempt the Lord your God. Never question God's faithfulness or seek public attention. Jesus never questioned God's faithfulness nor tempted God, but rather challenged Satan, who was tempting God. "And Jesus answere and said to him, It has been said, 'You shall not tempt the Lord thy God'" (Luke 4:12). **(P&P)**

40

Appropriating God's Power

Never fight the devil on your own strength. Be properly equipped. Do not fight the enemy without the proper equipment. "The name of the Lord is a strong tower; The righteous run to it and are safe." (Proverbs 18:10). Jesus did not send out his disciples without the proper equipment. Jesus was with them everywhere they

Guided by Wisdom

went. "After these things the Lord appointed seventy others also, and sent them two and two before His face into every city and place where He Himself was about to go" (Luke 10:1). They did not go in their own power. They went in the power of God, which was the power of Christ. "Behold, I send you out as lambs among wolves. He who hears you hears Me; he who reject you reject Me, and he who rejects Me rejects Him who sent Me" (Luke 10:3,16). "Behold, I send the promise of My Father upon you: but tarry in the city of Jerusalem, until you are endued with power from on high" (Luke 24:49).

When the disciples returned from their mission, Jesus was overjoyed at their success. "And He said to them, 'I saw Satan fall like lightning fall from heaven' (Luke 10:18).

Do not fight the enemy in your strength alone. You will go down in defeat if you do so. Apart from the Lord, you can do nothing. But with Him you can do all things. "I can do all things through Christ who strengthens me" (Philippians 4:13). It is only through the power of the blood of Jesus Christ that we have been given power and authority over Satan and his demons. "Behold, I give you the authority to trample on serpents and scorpions, and all over the power of the enemy, and nothing shall by any means hurt you" (Luke 10:19). "Put on the whole armor of God, that you may be able to stand against the wiles of the devil" (Ephesians. 6:11). As long as you remain in close fellowship with God, you will be given the power and authority needed to stand victoriously against Satan and his demons.

41

The Power of Consistency

Consistency is a powerful wisdom key. Consistency is a virtue. Be persistent. Prove the firmness of your Character. Without consistency, you can never be a good witness for God. The Word of God says, "I know your works, that you art neither cold nor hot. I could wish you were cold or hot. So then, because you are lukewarm, and neither cold nor hot, I will vomit you out of My mouth" (Revelation.3:15-16). Be consistent in faith, the Word, and holiness:

Consistency in Faith – Faith honors God, and God honors faith. "But without faith it is impossible to please Him, for he that comes to God must believe that He is, and that He is a rewarder of those that diligently seek him" (Hebrews 11:6). Abraham had consistency of faith. Regardless of circumstances he never wavered in his belief and faith in God. "For what does the scripture say? Abraham believed God, and it was counted to him for righteousness" (Romans 4:3). "Be steadfast in your faith, rooted and built up in Him" (Colossians 2:6 KJV).

Guided by Wisdom

Consistency in the Word - Do not be ignorant today as you were yesterday. That would mean negated consistency. You cannot become what you need to be by remaining what you are. Your ignorance of the word of God is the only effective weapon an enemy can use against you. Read the Word of God every day. The most valuable success habit in your life is your daily reading of the Word of God. The secret of your future is hidden in your daily routine. What you hear repeatedly you will eventually believe. God said to Joshua, "This book of the law shall not depart from your mouth, but you shall meditate in it day and night, that you may observe to do according to all that is written in it: for then you will make your way prosperous, and then you will have good success" (Joshua 1:8).

Reject your ignorance of God's Word. "Study to show thyself approved unto God, a workman that needed not to be ashamed, rightly dividing the word of truth" (2 Timothy 2:15, KJV). The Bible is designed to guide all who earnestly wish to become acquainted with the will of God. The Bible must be carefully and consistently studied with the humility of heart and prayers to obtain knowledge of God's will. By the aid of the Holy Spirit, which is promised to all who seek God in sincerity, every man or woman will understand the truth of the Word of God for himself or herself. The Spirit of Truth has been sent to guide men into all truth. Jesus Christ is the truth and the "light which gives light to every man coming into the world" (John 1:9). And upon the authority of the Son of God it is declared, "Ask, and it will be given to you;

Designed To Fight, Destined To Win

seek, and you will find; knock, and it will be opened to you: For everyone who asks receives, and he who seeks finds, and to him who knocks it will be opened" (Mathew 7:7-8). The only shield from delusion is the consistent study and searching of the Scriptures with contrition of soul and earnest prayer for divine guidance. "If anyone wills to do His will, he shall know concerning the doctrine, whether it is from God or whether I speak on My own authority" (John 7:17). The Word of God is plain to all who study it with prayerful heart. Every truly honest soul will come to the light of truth.

Consistency in Holiness - We are exhorted in the book of Hebrew to pursue holiness. "Pursue peace with all men, and holiness, without which no one will see the Lord" (Hebrew 12:14). We are called to be holy, just as He who called us is holy, so we must be holy in everything we do. "But as He who called you is holy, so also be holy in all your conduct, Because it is written, Be holy; for I am holy" (1 Peter 1:15:16). "But you are a chosen generation, a royal priesthood, and holy nation, His own special people, that you may proclaim the praises of him who called you out of darkness into his marvelous light "(1 Peter 2:9).   **(P&P)**

<u>Guided by Wisdom</u>

MEDITATION

1. If you can be bought, Satan can meet any price.

2. Do not be deceived by oratorical skills devoid of righteous living.

3. Prophesy your expected victory. "Death and life are in the power of the tongue, and those who love it will eat its fruit" (Proverbs 18:21).

4. The man who wins may have been counted out several times, but he didn't hear the referee.

5. Defeat never comes to any man until he admits it.

6. One of the marks of a winner is the ability to come back in an apparent defeat.

7. Great champions have all come back from an apparent defeat.

8. All men fall, but great men get back up again.

9. Whatever you are free from you are qualified for.

10. Whatever you abuse will eventually destroy you.

11. Whatever you compromise to gain you, will eventually lose

Designed To Fight, Destined To Win

12.   The secret of your future is hidden in your daily routine.

13.   What you hear repeatedly you will eventually believe.

14.   Do not be ignorant today as you were yesterday.

15.   You cannot become what you need to be by remaining what you are.

16.   Your ignorance of the word of God is the only effective weapon an enemy can use against you.

Guided by Wisdom

42

Expect Supernatural Intervention

When your availability meets with God, expect the supernatural. God does not ask for your ability but for your availability. Don't be afraid of the storm; master how to sail your ship. Your courage is developed by overcoming difficult times and adversity. When the enemy attacks you, God not only takes notice but gets involved. "Do not be afraid nor dismayed because of this great multitude, for the battle is not yours, but God's. ... You will not need to fight in this battle. Position yourselves, stand still, and see the salvation of the Lord who is with you" (2 Chronicles 20:15-17). When Daniel was thrown into the lion's Den, God intervened by shutting down the Lions mouth that they could not hurt him (see Daniel 6:10-23). When Shadrach, Meshach, and Abednego were thrown into the fiery furnace, God intervened by showing up in the fire, rendering the power of fire impotent against His servant. (Daniel 3:19-30). When God showed up, a slingshot from David killed Goliath. When God showed up, a rod from Moses' hand

Designed To Fight, Destined To Win

parted the Red Sea. When God showed up, one last pancake from the widow of Zarephath began her harvest. When God shows up on your behalf, who can stand against Him? **(P&P)**

43

Pain Is Temporal

Pain is not prejudice. Pain is a discomfort caused by disorder. Pain is a message you cannot ignore, regardless of the source, and there are a variety of sources. Pain is highly concentrated thought. Pain can be due to repressed emotions and negative reactions that were buried instead of faced and resolved. Pain can result due to: repressed fear, repressed anger, repressed anxiety, repressed frustration, repressed disappointment, repressed humiliation and other repressed toxic emotions. Never bury any toxic emotions. Deal with them forthrightly and get them resolved as quickly as possible to avoid adverse health consequences.

Pain can result due to never ending continuous streams of thoughts of negative outcome or consequences of the present or future undesired circumstances. These are thoughts injected into you from external satanic forces.

Guided by Wisdom

These thoughts must be continuously captured and replaced by what God says concerning the situation. Saturate your thought life with the Word of God continuously, rehearsing the Word day and night. There is nobody that has not felt the sting of pain.

Pain is inevitable but be mindful of what the pain is telling you concerning your health, relationships, finances, or any other areas of your life. Pain is temporal; it will pass away when order is reintroduced. Suffering or pain is a result some form of disorder in your life. Suffering or pain can be brought about by one form of impurity or another. When you purify yourself and reintroduce order into your life, the suffering will cease.

Pain is not always punishment. Pain can be a gateway to greater revelation of God. Pain or difficult times do not imply the absence of God. What you thought is dead, God can resurrect. The dream you thought is dead is about to be resurrected. The angel of the Lord said to Gideon, "The Lord is with you, you mighty man of valor" to which Gideon immediately replied, " If the Lord is with us, why then has all this happened to us? And where are all his miracles which our fathers told us about, saying, Did not the Lord bring us up from Egypt? But now the Lord has forsaken us, and delivered us into the hands of the Midianites." Then the Lord turned to him, and said, "Go in this might of yours, and you shall save Israel from the hand of the Midianites: have I not sent you" (Judges 6:12-16).

Designed To Fight, Destined To Win

Time does not heal. If time heals, medicine is unnecessary. If time heals, God is unnecessary. When God enters your life, order is reintroduced as you live your life by His precepts. Decisions you make today will impact every area of your life in the future. "And the Lord spoke to Manasseh and to his people, but they would not listen. Therefore the Lord brought upon them the captains of the army of the king of Assyria, who took Manasseh with hooks, bound him with bronze fetters, and carried him off to Babylon. Now when he was in affliction, he implored the Lord his God, and humbled himself greatly before the God of his fathers, And prayed to Him: and He received his entreaty, heard his supplication, and brought him back to Jerusalem into his kingdom. Then Manesseh knew that the Lord was God" (2 Chronicles 33:10-13). "Weeping may endure for a night, but joy comes in the morning" (Psalm 30:5). Forget the times of your distress, but never forget what they taught you. The depth of your adversity, determines the height of your successes. The harder you fall, the higher you bounce back. "For a righteous man may fall seven times, and rise up again, but the wicked shall fall by calamity" (Proverbs 24:16). **Gold is tried in the fire, but great men and women in the furnace of adversity. Adversity can cause some to break, others to break a record**. Decide to break the record. The path of least resistance is the path of the loser. "Those who sow in tears shall reap in joy" (Psalm 126:5).

When order is introduced, pain ceases. To reintroduce order to your life, "Acquaint now yourself with Him, and

Guided by Wisdom

be at peace: thereby good will come to you" (Job 22:21). People seek for good and prosperity first believing they will give them peace with Him, but the opposite is the truth. Seek God first and be at peace then good and prosperity will come to you. God's command to you is this: "If you diligently obey the voice of the Lord your God, to observe carefully all His commandments which I command you today, that the Lord your God will set you high above all nations of the earth: And all these blessings shall come upon you, and overtake you, because you obey the voice of the Lord your God: ... But it shall come to pass, if you do not obey the voice of the Lord your God, to observe carefully all His commandments and His status which I command you today, that all these curses will come upon you, and overtake you" (Deuteronomy 28:1-2,15).

From the beginning it was never God's intention for anybody to shade tears or cry. We were never meant to experience death, pain, sorrow or any of the evil vices we face today. All these vices came as a result of the fall of man. Disobedience to the law of God introduces disorder, which consequently results in evil vices. At the fullness of time, God will restore complete order, then all these demonic vices will cease. "And God will wipe away every tear from their eyes; there shall be no more death, nor sorrow, nor crying. There shall be no more pain, for the former things have passed away" (Revelation 21:4). **(P&P)**

44

Destined to Win

You are designed, built, supernaturally encoded, and destined to win. Your future is as bright as the promises of God so long as you are committed to obeying Him. The promise of success is embedded in your commitment to obedience. Understanding is hidden in obedience. It is your obedience that will unlock your understanding, but delayed obedience is disobedience. Obedience to God schedules seasons of success. Completion of instructions from God, schedules season of victory. Seasons of victory, successes, and promotions are scheduled each time God's instructions are completed.

God placed within you an unlimited wealth of resources. Utilize your talents today, and stop procrastinating. Don't let procrastination become your full-time occupation. Your talents will make a way for you in life. "A man's gift makes room for him, And brings him before great men" (Proverbs 18:16). Before you were born you were genetically pre-encoded with God's instructions and empowered to win. Your God given,

Guided by Wisdom

genetically encoded gifts, talents, abilities, and potentials are irreversible. They may be latent and dormant, yet they are there. **The ignorance of that which exists places limitation on that which is possible.**

Jeremiah was ordained a prophet before he was born. David was chosen and ordained to be king before he became the king many years later. Before Gideon received his assignment he was already a man of might. God said to Gideon, "Go in this might of yours, and you shall save Israel from the hand of the Midianites: Have I not sent you?" (Judges 6:14). When Gideon received his assignment, he said, "Oh my Lord, how can I save Israel? Indeed my clan is the weakest in Manasseh, and I am the least in my father's house" to which the Lord said, "...Surely I will be with you, and you shall defeat the Medianites as one man" (Judges 6:15-16). Before Jeremiah was born, he was already ordained a prophet. "Then the word of the Lord came to me, saying: Before I formed you in the womb I knew you; before you were born I sanctified you; I ordained you a prophet to the nations" (Jeremiah 1:4-5).

It is, however, your duty to recognize and develop your talents. You must find and develop your latent resources. The clue is in analyzing your major strengths, your driving force, and what you love to do even without pay. If you can do this and follow through with your destiny, you will be in exquisite poise. Dispel your paralyzing doubts, and have absolute confidence in God's Word. Vaccinate yourself against failure by invalidating all

Designed To Fight, Destined To Win

excuses based on inadequacy. It has been said that "attitude determines altitude" "Yet in all these things we are more than conquerors through Him that loved us" (Romans.8:37). Quit doubting yourself and believe God who created and empowered you. You are capable of more than you and others expect of you, even beyond your knowledge and most extravagant dreams. Your true strength and ability is not limited, reduced, or altered by the opinion of others or your previous experiences. Mediocrity is living below the purpose for which you were created. When you commit yourself and your plans to the Lord, He commits himself and His infinite resources to you. "Commit your way to the Lord; Trust also in Him; and He shall bring it to pass" (Psalm 37:5).

The obstacle between you and your dream may be laziness. The lazier you become, the more you plan to do tomorrow but tomorrow never ends. Lazy people are not world changers, though they can be parasites. Lazy people have no vision for the future. Lazy people can talk of their dreams but will not follow through. Lazy people have abundant "time" at their disposal to waste. Lazy people have abundant time to be poor. "A little sleep, a little slumber, A little folding of the hands to sleep So shall your poverty come on you like a prowler, And your need like an armed man" (Proverbs 6:10-11).   **(P&P)**

Guided by Wisdom

45

Reject Hatred Without Hating

Hatred is the anger of the weak and the ignorant. Hatred is an emotional poison of the soul. All haters are functioning under the devil's influence. They are agents of offense working for the devil. Hatred disunites human lives, fosters discrimination and hurls nations into ruthless and unnecessary war. In Hatred we see hell bound delusions, seas of tears, unimaginable wickedness, human carnage and torture, melancholy restrospection, telling of unspeakable anguish and grief, agonizing partings, untimely and unnatural deaths. "Woe to the world because of offenses! For offenses must come, but woe to that man by whom the offense comes!" (Matthew 18:7). When you hate someone, you love yourself less. Hatred toward someone is an indication of self hatred.

To hate someone is to be a God hater. You cannot be in right relationship with God and in wrong relationship with His children. If you think you can do that, you are simply deceived. If someone says, "I love God," and hates his brother, he is a liar; for he who does not love his

155

Designed To Fight, Destined To Win

brother whom he has seen, how can he love God whom he has not seen? He who says he is in the light, and hates his brother, is in darkness until now. Whoever hates his brother is a murderer, and you know that no murderer has eternal life abiding in him" (1 John 4:20; 2:9,;3:15) If you hate someone for any reason, God does not reside in you. God is love, and love is of God. You cannot give what you don't have. If you do not love, it is because God is not in you.

"Beloved, let us love one another, for love is of God; and everyone who loves is born of God and knows God. He who does not love does not know God, for God is love" (1 John 4:12). Refuse to give up because of hate. Jesus was hated by the Pharisees and rejected in His hometown of Nazareth, yet He fulfilled His assignment. (see Mathew12,13). Elijah was hated by Jezebel. (see 1 Kings 19). In the face of rejection and hate, you must move on stronger, not weaker; you must not allow rejection and hatred to beat you down. Instead let it strengthen your resolve on your assignment. Hatred does not cease by hatred but by love. It is written, "Do not be overcome by evil, but overcome evil with good" (Romans 12:21). "Seek good, and not evil, that you may live; So the Lord, the God of hosts, will be with you" (Amos.5:14). To seek good does not mean to entertain, to encourage, or to abate evil. Hating what God hates and loving what God loves puts you on the side of righteousness and justice. When you hate what God hates and love what God loves, you are obeying the Scriptures: "To fear the Lord is to hate evil" (Proverbs 8:13). You must reject evil. It is written,

Guided by Wisdom

"Hate evil, love good; Establish justice in the gate." (Amos 5:15). Let your heart expand and grow in love instead of hatred. Clinging to hatred deepens your wretchedness and delusion. Where hatred is, Love is not. Where love is, Hatred is not. Let your meditation expand with ever-broadening possibilities of tomorrow. Old things will pass away, and all things will become new. As a man thinks in his heart, so is he.

The scripture teaches against revenge. 'Vengeance is Mine, I will repay,' says the Lord.'" (Hebrews 10:30). Inflicting punishment or harm on another to pay back for an injury or insult should never be the lot of any Christian. Jesus taught that we should love our enemies (see Luke 6:27). **(P&P)**

46

Beware Of Your Associations

When the wrong people leave your life, right things happen. Be careful who you let into your life. When Satan wants to destroy your life, he sends a man or woman. There are four kinds of people. Some people add, some people subtract, some people divide, and some people multiply. People that subtract or divide will not increase you but decrease you. People that subtract or divide do not leave your life voluntarily. You must force them out or eat the fruit of their seed. Closing the door on them will initially be painful, but right things will happen when they leave. It is written, "Have no fellowship with the unfruitful works of darkness, but rather expose them. For it is a shameful even to speak of those things which are done by them in secret" (Ephesians 5:11-12).

When the disobedient Hebrew prophet sent to preach to Nineveh was thrown into the sea, there was calm in the sea. "So they picked up Jonah and threw him into the sea, and the sea ceased from its raging" (Jonah 1:15). When

Guided by Wisdom

Achan sinned by stealing part of the spoil, he brought trouble on his people. When Achan was killed because of his sin, the trouble ceased. "There is an accursed thing in your midst, O Israel; you cannot stand before your enemies until you take away the accursed thing from among you" (Joshua 7:13c, 7:1-25). "Do not be deceived: Evil company corrupts good habit." (1 Corinthians 15:33). "Come out from among them and be separate, says the Lord, Do not touch what is unclean, and I will receive you. I will be a Father to you, and you shall be My sons and daughters, Says the Lord Almighty." (1 Corinthians 6:17-18). "Make not friendship with an angry man; and with a furious man do not go: Lest you learn his ways, and set a snare for your soul" (Proverbs 22:24-25). "As charcoal is to burning coals, and wood to fire, so is contentious man to kindle strife" (Proverbs 26:21).

Be careful of your associations, your observations, what you see, what you taste, what you smell, what you feel, what you hear, what you touch, and your thought life. Refuse anything that does not agree with the word of God. Your thought life consists of what you have been taught, your thinking, disposition, observations, environment, and the people around you. You must therefore remove yourself or stay away from people, places, and things that do not agree with the Word of God; otherwise your faith can be negatively affected and contaminated. Besides, you can die because of wrong association. If you don't believe it, ask the shipmaster what happened to his ship when the disobedient Jonah

Designed To Fight, Destined To Win

was on board (Jonah 1:1-17;2:1-10). If you don't believe it, ask the Israelites what happened to them when Achan committed sin in their company against God (Joshua 7:1-25). **Your life is forced to the direction of your most dominant thought. Whatever dominates your attention determines the results you get.** Never think failure, never think doubt, never think victimized, but always think victorious because God cannot lie. "In hope of eternal life, which God, who cannot lie, promised before the time began" (Titus 1:2). "That by two immutable things, in which it was impossible for God to lie, we might have strong consolation, who have fled for refuge to lay hold upon the hope set before us" (Hebrews 6:18). Remember, it is written, "Therefore submit to God. Resist the devil and he will flee from you " (James 4:7). This means that you must be submitted to God first before the devil flees from you. If you are not submitted to God, the devil does not have to flee from you. **(P&P)**

Guided by Wisdom

47

Dare to Believe God

All things are possible if you dare to believe. Have faith in God. They that side with God always win. The wise man believes God and does not regard the small as too little nor the great as too big, because he knows there is no limit to what God can do. God is pleased when His Word is believed.

Jesus fed five thousand with five loaves and two fishes; David believed God and defeated Goliath with a sling. "Then David said to the Philistine, 'You come to me with a sword, with a spear, and with a javelin. But I come to you in the name of the Lord of host, the God of the armies of Israel, whom you have defied. This day the Lord will deliver you into my hand. Then all this assembly shall know that the Lord does not save with sword and spear: for the battle is the Lord's, and he will give you into our hands" (1 Samuel 17:45,47). "God is not a man, that he should lie; nor the son of man, that he should repent. Has He said, and will He not do it? Or has he spoken, and will He not make it good?" (Numbers 23:19). "Now faith is the substance of things hoped for, the evidence of things not seen. But without faith it is

Designed To Fight, Destined To Win

impossible to please him, for he who comes to God must believe that He is, and that He is a rewarder of them who diligently seek him" (Hebrews 11:1,6). **(P&P)**

48

False Accusation is the Last Stage Before a Supernatural Promotion

Satan uses false accusers to curse the righteous. All false accusers are liars like their father Satan. Joseph was promoted after being falsely accused by Pharaoh's wife (Genesis 39:1-23; 41:37-57). Daniel was promoted after the king's staff planned to exterminate him (Daniel 6:22-28). Do not respond in the flesh. Never respond until you have spent some time in the presence of God. False accusers are always exposed or judged. False accusers accuse to cover up their weaknesses. Accusations are sometimes believed, but be not afraid; get anchored on the Word of God. Whenever you are falsely accused, speak the truth according to God's Word. Remember, **your friends don't need your explanations,**

Guided by Wisdom

and your enemies will not believe your explanation. You don't need to convince your friends; they already believed you. You don't need to convince your enemies; they would not believe you. Just like Joseph, just like Daniel, your vindication is on the way! "For we know Him who said, Vengeance is Mine, I will repay, says the Lord. And again, The Lord will judge His people. It is a fearful thing to fall into the hands of the living God" (Hebrews 10:30-31). **(P&P)**

Designed To Fight, Destined To Win

MEDITATION

1. Gold is tried in the fire, but great men and women in the furnace of adversity.

2. Adversity can cause some to break, others to break a record.

3. Disobedience to the law of God introduces disorder, which consequently results in evil vices.

4. You are designed, built, supernaturally encoded, and destined to win.

5. Your future is as bright as the promises of God.

6. The promise of success is embedded in your commitment to obedience.

7. Your talents will make a way for you in life. "A man's gift makes room for him, And brings him before great men" (Proverbs 18:16).

8. Before you were born you were genetically pre-encoded with God's instructions and empowered to win.

9. The ignorance of that which exists places limitation on that which is possible.

Guided by Wisdom

10. You are capable of more than you and others expect of you, even beyond your knowledge and most extravagant dreams.

11. Your true strength and ability is not limited, reduced, or altered by the opinion of others or your previous experiences.

12. When you commit yourself and your plans to the Lord, He commits himself and His infinite resources to you.

13. Lazy people have abundant "time" at their disposal to waste.

14. Hatred is the anger of the weak and the ignorant.

15. When the wrong people leave your life, right things happen.

16. When Satan wants to destroy your life, he sends a man or woman.

17. Your life is forced to the direction of your most dominant thought.

18. Whatever dominates your attention determines the results you get.

19. Satan uses false accusers to curse the righteous.

Designed To Fight, Destined To Win

20. Your friends don't need your explanations, and your enemies will not believe your explanation. You don't need to convince your friends; they already believed you. You don't need to convince your enemies; they would not believe you.

Guided by Wisdom

49

Never Fear Your Enemy

Whatever you fear you will attract. Whatever you resist you will repel. Fear is a connector, just like faith is a connector. Fear connects you to the forces of evil. Fear will connect you to whatever you fear. A fear-based statement connected Job to the powers of darkness. Job said, "For the thing I greatly feared has come upon me, And what I dreaded has happened to me. I am not at ease, nor am I quiet; I have no rest, for trouble comes" (Job 3:25-26). Never make any fear-based decisions or statements.

Faith connects you to the forces of good. Faith will connect you to whatever you have faith for. Faith connected the woman with the issue of blood to her healing. "Your faith has made you well. Go in peace" (Luke 8:48).

A faith-based statement connected Peter to God. When Peter made the confession of faith, "You are the Christ, the Son of the living God," Jesus immediately said, "Blessed are you, Simon Bar-Jonah, for flesh and blood has not revealed *this* to you, but My Father who is in

Designed To Fight, Destined To Win

heaven. .. You are Peter, and on this rock I will build My church, and the gates of Hades shall not prevail against it. And I will give you the keys of the kingdom of heaven, and whatever you bind on earth will be bound in heaven, and whatever you loose on earth will be loosed in heaven" (Matthew 16-18). Doubt and fear are the enemies of success. Doubt and fear must be destroyed. Failure is conquered by destroying doubt and fear. Fear tolerated is faith contaminated. Fear is faith in reverse direction. Fear is a negated faith. Fear is faith in death. Fear comes by hearing, and hearing by the lies of the devil. Fear is the opposite of faith. Ungodly fear is born out of a negative experience of what happened to you or somebody else. Ungodly fear generates a negative expectation for the future.
Godly fear generates a positive expectation for the future.

Ungodly fear is not of God; ungodly fear is of the devil. Ungodly fear is the natural concomitance of the fall of man. Ungodly fear is the result of transgressing God's Law, coupled with the implosion bubble of evil and the wickedness of man. Instillation of fear is an antediluvian stratagem of the devil designed for his despicable murderous agenda. "For God has not given us a spirit of fear; but of power, and of love, and of sound mind" (2 Timothy 1:7). Ungodly fear is the spirit of bondage. "For you did not receive the spirit of bondage again to fear; but you received the Spirit of adoption, by whom we cry out, Abba, Father" (Romans 8:15). Begin to operate in the sphere of the wisdom of God, and look at things

Guided by Wisdom

through the lenses of His wisdom. Fear and panic dissipate in the face of wisdom, even if you are dipped into an unexpected valley or high on the pinnacle of prosperity. Wisdom provides, preserves, and protects objectivity and stability in the midst of any storm. No matter who you are and how confused you are about life, the wisdom of God will show you the meaning of life. Wisdom does not discriminate. No one is chosen, no one is rejected; you just have to seek wisdom with all your might.

Godly fear is wisdom, but the fear of man is the gate to hell. Godly fear connects you to God, but the fear of man connects you to the gates of hell. "The fear of the Lord is the beginning of wisdom."(Proverbs.9:10). "The fear of the Lord, that is wisdom" (Job 28:28). "The fear of the Lord is clean, enduring for ever; the judgments of the Lord are true and righteous altogether" (Psalm 19:9). "The fear of the Lord is to hate evil; Pride and arrogance and the evil way And the perverse mouth I hate" (Proverbs 8:13).

Everyone exists in submission to someone else. Those in authority do not necessarily have greater intelligence or gifts or skills, but they do have greater responsibility. Authority is established by God to deter evil, to inflict punishment on the law breakers, and to guide or develop by instruction. Submit to authority according to God's Word, but never submit to the control or manipulation of any man or woman. "For ye suffer, if a man bring you into bondage, if a man devour you, if a man take of you,

Designed To Fight, Destined To Win

if a man exalt himself, if a man smite you on the face" (2Corinthians 11:20, KJV). When any man or woman in authority resorts to control and manipulation, that man or woman has disqualified himself or herself from that position. The spirit of control and manipulation is of the devil. Obedience to God must precede obedience to men. Never obey men in violation of the Word of God. When man puts you up, he can put you down. When God puts you up, no man can put you down. When God promotes you, man can do nothing about it. "And now I say to you, keep away from these men and let them alone; for if this plan or this work is of men, it will come to nothing; but if it is of God, you cannot overthrow it - lest you even be found to fight against God" (Acts 5:38-39).

Don't think about things that will make you quit. Avoid dwelling on the negative. "Have I not commanded you? Be strong and of a good courage; Do not be afraid, nor be dismayed: for the Lord your God is with you wherever you go" (Joshua 1:9). "And do not fear those who kill the body, but cannot kill the soul: but rather fear Him who is able to destroy both soul and body in hell" (Matthew 10:28). Faith and fear operate through words. Words transmit power. Words reveal character. Words determine rewards and judgments. Words produce fruit. Words shapes destiny. Faith operates through the living words of God. The living words are words that agree with the Word of God. Fear operates through negated words. Negated words are words that do not agree with the Word of God.

Guided by Wisdom

Faith is not faith until words are spoken. It is the spoken word that powers faith. It is the spoken word that changes what you believe into the faith force. Faith force increases by the continuous hearing of the Word of God, with corresponding action. To increase your faith, speak the Word of God to your hearing continuously, with corresponding action. "So then faith comes by hearing, and hearing by the word of God" (Romans 10:17). Satan cannot operate in your life in the absence of fear. Resist fear; never manage fear, but rather cast it out. Perfect love casts out fear, and God is Love, and love never fails. Therefore, abide in God, and God will abide in you then your fear will dissipate. "There is no fear in love; but perfect love casts out fear, because fear involves torment. But he who fears has not been made perfect in love" (1John 4:18). "You will keep him in perfect peace, whose mind is stayed on You, because he trust in You. Trust in the Lord forever, For Yah, the LORD , is everlasting strength" (Isaiah 26:3).

Fear is not fear until words are spoken. It is the spoken word that powers fear. It is your words that gives fear power. Without your cooperation, fear has no power. When you refuse to feed your fear, it dies. Give fear no foothold in your life. To destroy fear in your life, refuse to speak negated words and refuse to hear negated words or bring up negated past experiences, and you have won already. Negated past experiences must be buried in the sea of forgetfulness. The devil uses negated past experiences, failures, pains, and disappointments to bring fear and doubt into your life to stop your future

Designed To Fight, Destined To Win

successes. Continuous rehearsal of the catalog of negative or bitter past experiences is contagious to your success. Refuse bringing up negated or bitter past experiences that must be forgotten. Refuse meditating on negative past experiences. Do not even talk about them. Talking about them gives them power to derail and frustrate your future successes.

Rehearse your victories and your successes. Meditate on the Word of God concerning your bright future based on the promises and provisions of the Word of God. Never meditate on anything that is not of good report. Anything that does not qualify for meditation does not qualify for your mind. Anything that does not qualify for your mind does not qualify for your mouth. Anything that does not qualify for your mouth does not qualify for conversation. That is why you must never make any fear-based prayers. When you say your prayers, pray in faith, not in fear. "Finally, brethren, whatsoever things are true, whatsoever things are noble, whatsoever things are just, whatsoever things are pure, whatsoever things are lovely, **whatsoever thing of good report**; if there is any virtue, and if there is anything praiseworthy, meditate on these things. The things which you learned, and received and heard and saw in me, do, and the God of peace will be with you" (Philippians 4:8-9).
Don't even discuss the flaws of other people to anybody. "I will return again to My place till they acknowledge their offense. Then they will seek My face; In their affliction they will earnestly seek Me" (Hosea 5;15).

(P&P)

172

Guided by Wisdom

50

Be not afraid of Sudden and Surprise Attack

Be not afraid of sudden attack. Be calm, collected, and calculated in the intense heat of the battle. The enemy will attack you at unexpected point and unexpected moments. To be passive is to run into great danger. Therefore you must always take the offensive. Next to victory, the act of pursuit is most important in war. The enemy's strongest weapon of offensive warfare is the surprise attack. This aggressor is well acquainted with this war; therefore, the less you know about his demonic devices, the greater the risks become. You must study to master his evil devices. You must study the word of God to master what God said about these devices. **Whatever you don't master will master you. Whatever you don't conquer will conquer you.**

The enemy specializes in subtle as well as surprise attacks. In a twinkle of an eye, without warning or preparation, the enemy can attack you. At other times, with subtle and insidious pressures, the enemy attacks.

Designed To Fight, Destined To Win

Be vigilant; be prepared to win. Do not panic. Listen to the voice of the Holy Spirit for direction. "Do not be afraid of sudden terror, nor of the trouble from the wicked when it comes. For the Lord will be your confidence, and will keep your foot from being caught" (Proverbs 3:25 26). Never utilize your spiritual weapons haphazardly, thereby losing some means of directing the battle. Utilize all spiritual weapons with the greatest audacity to fatigue and render the enemy impotent. You must amass uncommon knowledge of tactics, uncommon Methodism, and outstanding aptitude for the conduct of this battle. To accomplish the unforgettable, you must do the unpopular.   **(P&P)**

Guided by Wisdom

51

Pursue The Presence of God

Get into the presence of God. Never respond to your enemy until you have been in the presence of God. Take shelter in the presence of God. The Lord is your refuge, your habitation, your fortress, and your dwelling place. Abide under the shadow of the Almighty. In Him there is safety. Activate the presence of God through prayer, praise, and worship. That is what Righteous and Holy people do. Whenever you are in the presence of God, Satan must leave because he was officially evicted from the presence of God. The presence of God brings joy, peace, rest, security, blessing, power, wisdom, and vision. The presence of God will change your circumstances and bring victory over Satan.

"He who dwells in the secret place of the most High shall abide under the shadow of the Almighty. I will say of the Lord, He is my refuge and my fortress: my God; in Him I will I trust. ... Because you have made the Lord, who is my refuge, even the most High, your dwelling place, No

Designed To Fight, Destined To Win

evil shall befall you, nor shall any plague come near your dwelling. For He shall give his angels charge over you, to keep you in all your ways" (Psalm 91:1-2;9-11). "You will show me the path of life; In your presence is fullness of joy; at your right hand are pleasures forevermore" (Psalm 16:11). "And He said, My presence will go with you, and I will give you rest" (Exodus 33:14). "Then He arose, and rebuked the wind, and said unto the sea, 'Peace, be still!'. And the wind ceased, and there was a great calm" (Mark 4:39). "Blessed is the man You choose, And cause to approach You, That he may dwell in Your courts. We shall be satisfied with the goodness of Your house, or of your holy temple" (Psalm 65:4). "You shall hide them in the secret of Your presence from the plots of man; You shall keep them secretly in a pavilion from the strife of tongues" (Psalm 31:20). "For the weapon of our warfare are not carnal, but mighty in God for pulling down strongholds, Casting down arguments, and every high thing that exalts itself against the knowledge of God, bringing every thought into captivity to the obedience of Christ" (2 Corinthians 10:4-5).

"Wisdom is the principal thing; therefore get wisdom and in all your getting get understanding. Exalt her, and she will promote you: She will bring you honor, when you embrace her. She will place on your head an ornament of grace; A crown of glory she will deliver to you" (Proverbs 4:7-9). "Then Moses and the children of Israel sang this song to the Lord, and spoke, saying: 'I will sing to the Lord, For He has triumphed gloriously! The horse and its rider He has thrown into the sea! The Lord *is* my

Guided by Wisdom

strength and song, And He has become my salvation; He *is* my God, and I will praise Him; My father's God, and I will exalt Him. The Lord *is* a man of war; The Lord *is* His name. Pharaoh's chariots and his army He has cast into the sea; His chosen captains also are drowned in the Red Sea. The depths have covered them; They sank to the bottom like a stone. Your right hand, O Lord, has become glorious in power; Your right hand, O Lord, has dashed the enemy in pieces. And in the greatness of Your excellence You have overthrown those who rose against You; You sent forth Your wrath; It consumed them like stubble. And with the blast of Your nostrils The waters were gathered together; The floods stood upright like a heap; The depths congealed in the heart of the sea. The enemy said, "I will pursue, I will overtake, I will divide the spoil; My desire shall be satisfied on them. I will draw my sword, My hand shall destroy them." You blew with Your wind, The sea covered them; They sank like lead in the mighty waters. 'Who *is* like You, O Lord, among the gods? Who *is* like You, glorious in holiness, Fearful in praises, doing wonders? You stretched out Your right hand; The earth swallowed them" (Exodus 15:1-12).

(P&P)

52

Your Promotion is Scheduled

The enemy fights you the hardest when you are closest to your promised land and when you are next in line for promotion. You must fight back. Daniel was promoted after the lions den. Job received double blessing after his battle, Pharaoh made Joseph a ruler after the pit and the prison. David became king after defeating Goliath.

Don't run from the battle. Stay around for your crown. The award ceremony is the next scheduled event. "Therefore submit to God. Resist the devil, and he will flee from you" (James 4:7b). "Blessed is the man who endures temptation: for when he has been approved, he will receive the crown of life, which the Lord has promised to those who love Him" (James 1:12).

(P&P)

Guided by Wisdom

53

Resist the Devil

A nything you resist by your own power weakens you. Anything you resist by the power of God flees from you. Anything you yield yourself to empowers you positively or negatively. Choose wisely. Your greatest weakness can stop your greatest desire.

When you live your life for God, you are empowered against the devil and his legion of demons. Satan has no option but to leave when he is firmly resisted. Joseph resisted the devil that enticed him through Potiphar's wife (Genesis 39:7-23). Every temptation, every opposing influence, whether open or secret, must be successfully resisted. "Neither give place to the devil" (Ephesians 4:27 KJV). "Not by might, nor by power, but by my Spirit, says the Lord of hosts" (Zechariah 4:6). Neither the devil nor wicked men can hinder the work of the Almighty God. "For the eyes of the Lord are on the righteous, and His ears are open to their prayers: but the face of the Lord is against those who do evil. And who is he who will harm you, if you become followers of what is good?" (1 Peter 3:12-13). You must with subdued, contrite heart,

Designed To Fight, Destined To Win

confess and put away your sins, and in faith claim Gods promises. "For sin shall not have dominion over you" (Romans 6:14). "This I say, therefore, and testify in the Lord, that you should no longer walk as rest of the Gentiles walk, in the futility of their mind, Having the understanding darkened, being alienated from the life of God because of the ignorance that is in them, because of the blindness of their heart" (Ephesians 4:17-18). "Sin is a reproach to any people" (Proverbs 14:34). "But fornication, and all uncleanness, or covetousness, let it not even be named among you, as is fitting for saints; neither filthiness, nor foolish talking, nor coarse jesting, which are not fitting, but rather giving of thanks. For this you have known, that no fornicator, unclean person, nor covetous man, who is idolater, has any inheritance in the kingdom of Christ and God. Let not one deceive you with empty words, for because of these things the wrath of God comes upon the sons of disobedience. Therefore do not be partakers with them. For you were once darkness, but now you are light in the Lord. Walk as children of light for the fruit of the Spirit is in all goodness, righteousness, and truth, finding out what is acceptable to the Lord. And have no fellowship with the unfruitful works of darkness, but rather expose them" (Ephesians 5:3-11).

When Balaam, allured by the promise of rich reward from Balak, the king of the Moabites, practiced enchantments against Israel, and by sacrifice to the Lord sought to invoke a curse upon Israel, the Lord forbade the evil that Balaam longed to pronounce, forcing Balaam to

Guided by Wisdom

declare "How shall I curse whom God has not cursed? And how shall I denounce whom the Lord has not denounced?" (Numbers 23:8). "Let me die the death of the righteous, and let my last end be like his!" (Numbers 23:10). This wish was never granted. He had come to curse Israel but now desired to share in Israel's blessing. Balaam knew he was not suppose to curse the Israelites, but when Balak beefed up his reward, a second sacrifice was offered, and the pagan prophet exclaimed, "Behold, I have received commandment to bless: and He has blessed, and I cannot reverse it. He has not observed iniquity in Jacob, nor has He seen wickedness in Israel. The Lord his God is with him and the shout of a king is among them. For there is no sorcery against Jacob. Nor any divination against Israel: It now must be said of Jacob and of Israel, 'Oh, what God has done!" (Numbers 23:20-21,23). "God is not a man, that He should lie; nor a son of man, that He should repent. Has He said, and will He not do it? or has He spoken, and will He not make it good?" (Numbers 23:19). A third sacrifice was offered, and the pagan prophet essayed to secure a curse. The Spirit of the Lord entered him, and from the unwilling lips of the prophet, the Spirit of God declared prosperity on Israel and rebuked the folly and malice of their foes: "Blessed is he who blesses you, and cursed is he who curses you" (Numbers.24:9). Balaam instead of cursing the Israelites, fulfilled God's promises to Abraham with his own words, "I will bless those who bless you, and I will curse him who curses you" (Geneis 12:3). Balaam, prophesied, that the Israelites would be innumerable, echoing God's direct word to make

Designed To Fight, Destined To Win

Abraham's "seed as the dust of the earth" (Genesis 13:16,KJV).

So long as the Israelites were in complete loyalty and obedience to God, no power in earth or hell could prevail against them. But when the Moabites seduced Israel into sin, a plague came against the Israelites, destroying 24,000 people. When they transgressed God's commandment, they separated themselves from God, the veil was lifted, and they were left to the power of the destroyer. Satan is well aware that when you abide in Christ, he has no power over you. It is only in complete reliance upon God, and obedience to all His commandments that you can be secure. Therefore, heed the holy writ, "Therefore submit to God. Resist the devil, and he will flee from you. Draw near to God, and He will draw near to you" (James 4:7-8).   **(P&P)**

Guided by Wisdom

54

Protect Your Dreams

Keep your enemy off-balance and in the dark concerning your dreams. They cannot sabotage your dreams if they don't have a clue what you are up to and by the time they realize your intentions, it will be too late for them to stage sabotage. Never share your dreams with your enemy, Never show your enemy your treasures because of one simple act of kindness. Doing so could trigger adverse, unintended consequences. When Hezekiah showed Merodach, King of Babylon, all his treasures because of a simple act of kindness, the Word of the Lord came to Hezekiah saying, "Behold, the days are coming when all that *is* in your house, and what your fathers have accumulated until this day, shall be carried to Babylon; nothing shall be left" (Isaiah 39:6).

The source of a gift or kindness determines the motive behind that gift or kindness. Never receive any gift that will cost you your freedom. Sometimes, to receive a gift is to lose your freedom. Be careful what you receive and from whom. A gift blinds the wise and perverts the words of the righteous. "And thou shalt take no gift: for the gift

183

Designed To Fight, Destined To Win

blindeth the wise, and perverteth the words of the righteous" (Exodus 23:8,KJV). Your enemy can give in order to entrap. A gift may be an entrapment or a sign or repentance. What is your enemy giving you? Kindness or snare? Gift or snare? You decide!

Your enemy can use your word against you. "Then the king said to the man of God, 'Come home with me and refresh yourself, and I will give you a reward' But the man of God said to the king, 'If you were to give me half your house, I would not go in with you; nor would I eat bread nor drink water in this place. For so it was commanded me by the word of the Lord, saying, "You shall not eat bread, nor drink water, nor return by the same way you came"' .... and went after the man of God, and found him sitting under an oak. Then he said to him, 'Are you the man of God who came from Judah?' And he said, 'I *am.*' Then he said to him, 'Come home with me and eat bread.' And he said, 'I cannot return with you nor go in with you; neither can I eat bread nor drink water with you in this place. For I have been told by the word of the Lord, 'You shall not eat bread nor drink water there, nor return by going the way you came.'"
He said to him, 'I too *am* a prophet as you *are,* and an angel spoke to me by the word of the Lord, saying, 'Bring him back with you to your house, that he may eat bread and drink water.'" (He was lying to him.) When he was gone, a lion met him on the road and killed him. And his corpse was thrown on the road, and the donkey stood by it. The lion also stood by the corpse" (1 King 13:7-9; 14-18, 24)

Guided by Wisdom

Saul gave to David, hoping to kill him through the gift. Saul gave his daughter Michal to David, hoping to use her to entangle and snare him. "So Saul said, 'I will give her to him, that she may be a snare to him, and that the hand of the Philistines may be against him" (1 Samuel 18:21).

Never discuss your problems with your enemy. Sometimes things should be worked out behind the scene rather than in public view. There is really no use telling people about your problems, because you will find out that half of the people don't care and the other half are glad that you have those problems.   **(P&P)**

Designed To Fight, Destined To Win

55

Make Use of What You Have

Never complain of what you didn't have, make use of what you do have. When Moses found himself and the Israelites in danger between the Egyptian army and the Red Sea, God used what Moses had in his hand to deliver them. Moses held a staff or rod in his hand, and God used it to part the Red Sea (see Exodus 14:1-31). David killed Goliath with a slingshot (see 1 Samuel 17). One last pancake from the widow of Zarephath began her harvest (see 1 Kings 17:1-24). Elisha struck the Syrians blind by a prayer to God (2 Kings 6:16-19). Make sure you are under the will of God for your life. When you have God, you have everything.

Make sure you are obedient to God's instructions. **Obedience to God's instructions guarantees provision.** When God sends you, He will meet your needs. When God sent Elijah to Zarephath, He commanded a widow woman there to sustain him. When God sent Elijah to the Brook Cherith, He commanded the ravens to feed him

Guided by Wisdom

there. When God's power meets with what you have, victory is guaranteed.

When you recognize and use what you have, the tide of the battle will turn in your favor and something gloriously wonderful will happen in your life. Then you will know that, "The LORD does not save with sword and spear; for the battle *is* the LORD's" (1 Samuel 17:47). The Lord God Himself will become an adversary to your enemy. "I will rebuke the devourer for your *sakes*" (Malachi 3:11). The Holy Spirit will demoralize and weaken your enemy with fear towards you. He did that for the Israelites, as we see when Rahab said to the men, "I know that the Lord has given you the land, that the terror of you has fallen on us, and that all the inhabitants of the land are fainthearted because of you. And as soon as we heard *these things,* our hearts melted; neither did there remain any more courage in anyone because of you, for the Lord your God, He *is* God in heaven above and on earth beneath" (Joshua 2:9,11).　　　　**(P&P)**

Designed To Fight, Destined To Win

MEDITATION

1. You can't take a vacation in hell to see how you like it.

2. Whatever you fear you will attract. Whatever you resist you will repel.

3. Fear tolerated is faith contaminated. Fear is faith in reverse direction. Fear is a negated faith. Fear is faith in death.

4. Fear is a connector, just like faith is a connector. Fear connects you to the forces of evil. Faith connect you to the forces of good.

5. Godly fear is wisdom, but the fear of man is the gate to hell.

6. Faith is not faith until words are spoken.

7. Fear is not fear until words are spoken.

8. Doubt and fear are the enemies of success.

9. Failure is conquered by destroying doubt and fear.

10. Fear tolerated is faith contaminated. Fear is faith in reverse direction. Fear is a negated faith. Fear is faith in death.

Guided by Wisdom

11. Whatever you don't master will master you. Whatever you don't conquer will conquer you.

12. The enemy's strongest weapon of offensive warfare is the surprise attack.

13. Anything you resist by your own power weakens you. Anything you resist by the power of God flees from you.

14. Anything you yield yourself to empowers you positively or negatively.

15. Never share your dreams with your enemy.

16. Never show your enemy your treasures because of one simple act of kindness.

17. The source of a gift or kindness determines the motive behind that gift or kindness.

18. Never receive any gift that will cost you your freedom. Sometimes, to receive a gift is to lose your freedom.

19. Never discuss your problems with your enemy.

56

Defining Who You Are

God's greatness is often fertilized in human weakness. When you recognize that you are not what you did, then your deliverance is near. You are much better than what you did. Never allow your past mistakes to define who you are. What you did is not you. **Never live out your destiny based on what people call you**. Do not let words spoken over you by other people silence the gift inside you. No man or woman can devalue what God has set you to be. Never buy into what people call you. Do not agree with the labels being forced on you by other people. It has been said that only tailors behave sensibly: they take your measurements anew each time you go to them. The rest of the people go on with your old measurements and expect you to fit them. Refuse any negative tags placed on you by other people. Never allow an experience to be a definition. People can give you a name based on a single incident. Refuse to be defined by those names. You are not what you did. Yes, you did that, but that is not really who you are. You must define yourself with something other than your past. You are not so damaged that you cannot recover. You are not too young or too old for your purpose in life. Remember,

Guided by Wisdom

behavior permitted is behavior perpetuated. Yesterday is gone, today is a new day, tomorrow may never be there, therefore live for today and never try to put a question mark where God has already put a period.

The mercy of God is fresh and new every day. Only God can show you who you truly are. Only God can tell you your real name. "The Lord hath called me from the womb; from the matrix of my mother He has made mention of my name" (Isaiah 49:1). God told Jacob his real name. God called Jacob Israel, yet Jacob was a con man. God used Moses to deliver the children of Israel out of bondage, yet Moses was a murderer. God called David a man after His own heart, yet David was a murderer and an adulterer. Abraham was a liar, yet God made him the father of many nations. Peter struck Malchus, cutting off his right ear, yet Peter ignored his mistakes, was filled with the Holy Ghost, and preached the first Pentecostal sermon (Act 2.1-47). Peter repented after denying Jesus Christ three times and became one of the pillars of the Church, but Judas refused to repent and instead committed suicide. All men fall, but great men get back up again. "For a righteous man may fall seven times, and rise again, but the wicked shall fall by calamity" (Proverbs 24:16). **(P&P)**

Designed To Fight, Destined To Win

57

Respect Is Reciprocal

Whatever you respect you will attract. Whatever you disrespect you will repel. Whatever you fear, you will attract, and whatever you resist you will repel. To disrespect something or someone is to lose respect from that person. You cannot do wrong without suffering wrong. Respect is reciprocal. Always treat people the way you want to be treated. Treat people with dignity, respect, understanding, and trust. Deal with people who treat you otherwise with wisdom.

Respect those in authority. Authority is established by God to hinder evil, to chastise the law breakers, to direct and develop people by instruction. When you respect those in authority, you are respecting the office they occupy. Authority prevents disorder and creates order. Absence of authority creates chaos. Without authority society will be in turmoil, families in unruliness, the military in disarray, the schools in anarchy, and the whole world in pandemonium.

Guided by Wisdom

"Let every soul be subject to the governing authorities. For there is no authority except from God, and the authorities that exist are appointed by God. Therefore whoever resists the authority resists the ordinance of God, and those who resist will bring judgment on themselves. For rulers are not a terror to good works, but to evil. Do you want to be unafraid of the authority? Do what is good, and you will have praise from the same. For he is God's minister to you for good. But if you do evil, be afraid; for he does not bear the sword in vain; for he is God's minister, an avenger to *execute* wrath on him who practices evil" (Romans 13:4). "Therefore submit yourselves to every ordinance of man for the Lord's sake, whether to the king as supreme, or to governors, as to those who are sent by him for the punishment of evildoers and *for the* praise of those who do good. For this is the will of God, that by doing good you may put to silence the ignorance of foolish men— as free, yet not using liberty as a cloak for vice, but as bondservants of God. Honor all *people.* Love the brotherhood. Fear God. Honor the king" (1 Peter 2:13-17)

Submission to authority does not mean disobedience to God. Any order that is in direct conflict with God's command should not be obeyed. Fools take to themselves the respect that is given to the office they occupy. When those in authority abuse that authority, they lose the respect of the office they occupy. To abuse authority is to introduce disorder in the chain of command. There is a gradation among hierarchies, and this gradation exists

Designed To Fight, Destined To Win

even in the heavenly realm. Anyone in authority who
introduces disorder in the chain of command is not
worthy of the office and the authority they hold. When
Satan attempted to introduce disorder in the Kingdom of
God's hierarchy, he was forcefully evicted and thrown
out of the command chain. Those in authority who are
plotting to destroy you unjustly will be destroyed. Haman
abused his authority by plotting to destroy the Jews but
was instead destroyed himself. (see Esther 3,4,5,6,7,8).
Ahab, King of Israel, and Jezebel his wife abused their
authority and consequently died. Jezebel determined to
destroy Elijah the man of God because of her evil
disposition (see 1 King 19:2). When Naboth refused to
give Ahab his vineyard, which was his father's
inheritance, Jezebel conspired to kill Naboth to take the
vineyard. Ahab's willing compliance with Jezebel's
scheme to confiscate Naboth's vineyard made him guilty
of murder and theft. And God said to Ahab, "In the place
where dogs licked the blood of Naboth, dogs shall lick
your blood, even yours" (1 Kings 21:19b). And to Jezebel
the Lord said, "The dogs shall eat Jezebel by the wall of
Jezreel" (1 Kings 21:23).

'Thus says the Lord God: 'Because the Philistines dealt
vengefully and took vengeance with a spiteful heart, to
destroy because of the old hatred,' therefore thus says the
Lord God: 'I will stretch out My hand against the
Philistines, and I will cut off the Cherethites and destroy
the remnant of the seacoast. I will execute great
vengeance on them with furious rebukes; and they shall

Guided by Wisdom

know that I *am* the Lord, when I lay My vengeance upon them.' "(Ezekiel 25:15-17).

Treat the Word of God with a profound awe and respect. "Therefore, since we are receiving a kingdom which cannot be shaken, let us have grace, by which we may serve God acceptably with reverence and godly fear. For our God *is* a consuming fire" (Hebrews 12:28-29).

Treat yourself and others with respect. You are fearfully and wonderfully made. "I will praise You, for I am fearfully *and* wonderfully made; Marvelous are Your works, And *that* my soul knows very well" (Psalm 139:14). "What is man that You are mindful of him, And the son of man that You visit him? For You have made him a little lower than the angels, And You have crowned him with glory and honor" (Psalm 8:4-5).

If you respect yourself, you will never allow anybody to intimidate, dominate, manipulate, coerce, or control you. When you allow people to intimidate, dominate, manipulate, coerce or control you, you lose your respect and your ability to lead. Nobody follows anyone they can intimidate, dominate, manipulate, or control. To tolerate disrespect is to water the seeds of destruction. The disrespect you tolerated today is your tomorrow's warfare.

The anointing you respect is the anointing you will attract. The anointing you disrespect is the anointing you will repel. Elisha respected Elijah's anointing;

Designed To Fight, Destined To Win

consequently he took up Elijah's mantle with a double portion of his anointing (see 2 Kings 2:9-12). Gehazi disrespected the anointing on Elisha and received a curse instead of a blessing. (see 2 Kings 5:27). **(P&P)**

58

Identify Your Purpose

Purpose is highly concentrated, passionate thought towards an end to be attained, backed by plans and actions. Purpose will motivate you. Purpose will keep your priorities straight. Purpose will develop your potential. Purpose will empower you to live in the present, not in the past. Purpose will enable you to evaluate your progress. Attitude always determines altitude. Therefore, you must govern your actions and guard your attitude as it relates to your purpose.

What is your purpose? Success is doing daily God's purpose for your life. You won't be satisfied until you are doing God's purpose or assignment for your life. The secure place to be is in the will of God. God's purpose for your life is greater than you; therefore, you lose the right to think only about yourself. You must continuously look

Guided by Wisdom

ahead to remain steadfast in your purpose. There are others who cannot start until you start your purpose. In other words, other people's purpose may depend on your purpose. Can God count on you to fulfill your purpose? Can you be trusted? Aimlessness is weakness, but concentration is power. Your chief end is to glorify God in your purpose and enjoy Him forever. Make sure what you are living for is worth dying for. You are only as strong as your purpose. When you surrender to your purpose, your joy is fulfilled and you will have good days wherever you go. When you surrender to your circumstances, your joy will be unfulfilled, and then you will have good days and bad days.

It is not how busy you are, but why you are busy. Be not simply good; be good for something. He who can't stand for something will fall for anything. Unsuccessful people think merely of spending time, successful people think of using time. Multitudes of people are drifting aimlessly to and fro without a defined set and determined purpose, in that they deny themselves the fulfillment of their capacities and the satisfying happiness that attends it. Without purpose you will wander into the morass of dissatisfaction, but with purpose you will harness your abilities, and in your abilities is rich compensation. Purpose simplifies life and concentrates abilities, and concentration adds power. The meaning of life is to give life meaning. The aim of life is the best defense against death. There is no business in life but your supreme purpose and assignment. Your purpose should be the centralizing point of your conduct and thought life. Your

Designed To Fight, Destined To Win

purpose is your supreme assignment. Each act of yours makes a statement concerning your purpose. Those devoid of central purpose in their lives will always fall prey to self-pity, fear, trouble, and worries, which indicate weakness and leads to loss, unhappiness, and failure. You should be focused and concentrated on apprehension of your purpose.

Pursue your purpose bravely defying the storm. The storm of many falls, the storm of ingratitude, the storm of slander, the storm of many wounds, the storm of back-stabbers, the storm of betrayal, the storm of unfriendly friends and the storm of evil plotters. Surely victory is here even in the midst of the storm. Every fall, wound, betrayal and slip is a lesson learned, an experience gained from which wisdom leading unmistakably toward freedom is extracted. Never let any single or even multiples of incidents stop you. Failure at any point should never stop your progress. The process of success comes through repeated failures with unshakeable resolve not to quit when the going gets tough. Be aware though that skills and strength can only be developed by active will, effort, constant practice, and repetition. You will make incremental progress towards your goal by adding effort to effort, practice to practice, and repetition to repetition with an undeniable, concentrated focus. The strength of every effort is the measure of its result. The fruit of effort is the achievement.

If you wait for the provision to show up before you start your purpose, you might as well forget it. It is not what

Guided by Wisdom

you don't have that keeps you from reaching your goal; it's what you think you need. Don't be overcome with frustration when you encounter a problem or are waiting for your resources or provisions. When you start your purpose, the provision will show up. When you start your purpose, you will discover that your provision is incorporated into your purpose. Every God-given purpose has a built-in provision. Provision is hidden in your purpose, and prosperity is only guaranteed in your purpose. Whatever you were born to do will attract whatever is needed to do it. Aimlessness must be exterminated in your life for progress to be made in the right direction. Put away aimlessness and be consumed by the passion of your purpose. Be concentrated, attempt fearlessly, and accomplish masterfully.

Everyone has a consummate dream of the best level of human existence. Everyone has a common desire for the best life attainable. But not everyone has the commitment and concentration needed to make it happen. To succeed you must plan masterfully. Failing to plan is planning to fail. Failing to prepare is preparing to fail. To willingly commit sin is planning to fail. Deliberately planned sin leads to weakness, failure, unhappiness, and loss because weakness cannot persist in a power-evolving universe. Everything there is, was one time only a dream. If you cherish a dream, a vision, a lofty ideal, you will one day realize it if you don't let go of the dream. You may not cherish what you don't desire, but you will always cherish what you do desire. When you desire, you will obtain. When you aspire, you will achieve. I encourage

Designed To Fight, Destined To Win

you to dream big dreams, and as you dream, so must you become. **Men and women of vision make today serve tomorrow**. The visions of yesteryears are serving us today. So will the vision of today serve our tomorrows and our aftermath.

How to reach your goal:

1. You need a clear picture of what you want to accomplish.
2. You need an intense passionate desire to accomplish that goal.
3. You must be confident. Your confidence must be based on God. Reflect on your past victories and on your relationship with the Almighty God.
4. You need a planed course of action.
5. You must depend on the Holy Spirit for guidance.
6. You need a calendar of event. Set schedule and target dates.
7. You need cooperation
8. You must be consistent
9. You must control your emotion
10. You need the courage to act
11. You need a conscious dependence on God.
12. Expect reward. **(P&P)**

Guided by Wisdom

MEDITATION

1. Do not let words spoken over you by other people silence the gift inside you. No man or woman can devalue what God has set you to be.

2. Behavior permitted is behavior perpetuated.

3. Whatever you respect you will attract.

4. Whatever you disrespect you will repel.

5. Whatever you fear, you will attract, and whatever you resist you will repel.

6. To disrespect something or someone is to lose respect from that person.

7. Anyone in authority who introduces disorder in the chain of command is not worthy of the office and the authority they hold.

8. To tolerate disrespect is to water the seeds of destruction.

9. The disrespect you tolerated today is your tomorrow's warfare.

10. The anointing you respect is the anointing you will attract.

Designed To Fight, Destined To Win

11. Purpose is highly concentrated, passionate thought towards an end to be attained, backed by plans and actions.

12. Success is doing daily God's purpose for your life.

13. Aimlessness is weakness, but concentration is power.

14. Be not simply good; be good for something.

15. He who can't stand for something will fall for anything.

16. Unsuccessful people think merely of spending time, successful people think of using time.

17. The meaning of life is to give life meaning.

18. The aim of life is the best defense against death.

19. You will make incremental progress towards your goal by adding effort to effort, practice to practice, and repetition to repetition with an undeniable, concentrated focus.

20. The strength of every effort is the measure of its result.

Guided by Wisdom

21. The fruit of effort is the achievement.

22. If you wait for the provision to show up before you start your purpose, you might as well forget it.

23. Provision is hidden in your purpose, and prosperity is only guaranteed in your purpose.

24. Whatever you were born to do will attract whatever is needed to do it.

25. Failing to plan is planning to fail. Failing to prepare is preparing to fail.

26. Men and women of vision make today serve tomorrow.

59

Forgive Totally and Completely

You must forgive totally and completely. They who forgive shall be forgiven, but they who do not forgive shall not be forgiven. Christ has plainly warned us that if we do not forgive men their trespasses, neither will God forgive ours (Mathew 6:15). "Whatever a man sows, that he will also reap" (Galatians 6:7). Yes, you were unfairly hurt. Yes, you did not deserve the deep hurt. Yes, you did not deserve the disloyalty and betrayal. Yes, they don't even care. Yes, they are clueless of the hurt they have caused. Yes, they are happy for the hurt they have caused you. Yes, those who hurt you are already dead. What am I suppose to do now, you might ask. You must forgive totally and completely. Sometimes, life can be very unbearably unfair, yet love's power to forgive will heal you and set your future course in order. Forgiving is the only power that can stop the inexorable stream of painful memories. Forgiveness is God's command that oils relationships. *"Be angry, and do not sin*: do not let the sun go down on your wrath, nor give

Guided by Wisdom

place to the devil" (Ephesians 4:26-27). "Let all bitterness, wrath, anger, clamor, and evil speaking be put away from you, with all malice. And be kind to one another, tenderhearted, forgiving one another, even as God in Christ forgave you" (Ephesians 4:31-32).

Forgiveness is the attribute of the strong. The weak cannot forgive. The brave and the winners rebuke and forgive, but losers play passive with unforgiveness. Forgiveness heals the hurts you don't deserve. Unforgiveness prevents healing. Contemplation of revenge keeps the wounds alive that otherwise would heal. Reclaim your happiness by forgiving and getting the consequent healing from the burden of hurt you don't deserve. When you forgive you liberate yourself from self-imposed shackles. Forgiveness will not change the past; rather it releases you to go on with your life. Forgive yourself and others all the faults and mistakes, and then move on with your life.
Nothing makes you more unfit for the pursuit of holiness than a resentful and unforgiving spirit. Angry passions, the spirit of unforgiveness and revenge disqualify you from worshiping God, from showing up in the presence of God, from rendering profitable service to your fellows in honor of the Almighty God, and disqualify your gifts and sacrifice to God. Unforgiveness can send you to hell. Be wise!

Forgiveness is not tolerating the unfair, wicked, and diabolical act meted to you. Forgive, but never tolerate the unfair, wicked, and diabolical act. **You can forgive**

Designed To Fight, Destined To Win

anything, but you cannot tolerate everything. To tolerate everything is to sign in for a lot of trouble God never intended for you to be in. God never commanded you to tolerate everything! Never get forgiving mixed up with tolerance. You don't have to tolerate what people do just because you forgive them for doing it. Forgiving heals you personally, but tolerating everything will only hurt you in the long run.

You must forgive totally and completely! "For if you forgive men their trespasses, your heavenly Father will also forgive you. But if you do not forgive men their trespasses, neither will your Father forgive your trespasses" (**Matthew 6:14–15**).

"Then Peter came to Him and said, 'Lord, how often shall my brother sin against me, and I forgive him? Up to seven times?' Jesus said to him, 'I do not say to you, up to seven times, but up to seventy times seven. Therefore the kingdom of heaven is like a certain king who wanted to settle accounts with his servants. And when he had begun to settle accounts, one was brought to him who owed him ten thousand talents. But as he was not able to pay, his master commanded that he be sold, with his wife and children and all that he had, and that payment be made. The servant therefore fell down before him, saying, "Master, have patience with me, and I will pay you all." Then the master of that servant was moved with compassion, released him, and forgave him the debt.

Guided by Wisdom

'But that servant went out and found one of his fellow servants who owed him a hundred denarii; and he laid hands on him and took *him* by the throat, saying, "Pay me what you owe!" So his fellow servant fell down at his feet and begged him, saying, "Have patience with me, and I will pay you all." And he would not, but went and threw him into prison till he should pay the debt. So when his fellow servants saw what had been done, they were very grieved, and came and told their master all that had been done. Then his master, after he had called him, said to him, "You wicked servant! I forgave you all that debt because you begged me. Should you not also have had compassion on your fellow servant, just as I had pity on you?" And his master was angry, and delivered him to the torturers until he should pay all that was due to him. "So My heavenly Father also will do to you if each of you, from his heart, does not forgive his brother all trespasses" **(Matt 18:21–35).**

The power of the Almighty God working in you will enable you to attempt the unthinkable, endure the unbearable, forgive the unforgivable, and accomplish infinitely more than you would ever dare to ask or think. "Now to Him who is able to do exceedingly abundantly above all that we ask or think, according to the power that works in us, to Him be glory in the church by Christ Jesus to all generations, forever and ever. Amen" (Ephesians 3:20).   **(P&P)**

60

Resist Anxiety, Don't Worry, Be Happy

Worry is a distrust of God's providence. Worrying about the future evidences a distrust of divine providence and a doubting of God's goodness. When you believe that nothing will happen to you apart from that which God allows, then you can turn loose of the cares that hold you captive on the roadway of life. God promised peace to you if you turn away from your wicked ways and live a holy life. God's kind of peace does not panic in the face of any storm.

Worry does not empty tomorrow of its sorrow; it empties today of its strength. Worry never fixes anything. Worry exposes those things over which you have no authority. **Whatever you worry about, you have no authority over.** The good new is, though you have no authority over whatever you worry about, yet in Christ you do. You must stand in the authority of Christ and His anointing. Christ means The anointed One and His anointing. The anointing is the burden-removing yoke-destroying power

Guided by Wisdom

of God. Jesus said, "All authority has been given to Me in heaven and in earth" (Mathew 28:18). "Having disarmed principalities and powers, He made a public spectacle of them, triumphing over them in it" (Colossians 2:15). Jesus said, "Behold, I give unto you the authority to trample on serpents and scorpions, and over all the power of the enemy, and nothing shall by any means hurt you. These signs will follow those who believe: In My name they will cast out demons; they will speak with new tongues; they will take up serpents; and if they drink any deadly thing, it will by no means hurt them; they will lay hands on the sick, and they will recover" (Luke 10:19; Mark 16:17-18). This is the transfer of power into your hand. If you abide in Christ, which is to abide in the Word of God and live your life as the Scripture says, and if you do not let the Word depart from you, you have the authority, power, and anointing required for defeating the enemy. If you abide in the anointed One and His anointing then the Burden-removing, yoke-destroying power of God resides in you.

You can turn from fear and anxiety to faith and peace in the power of Christ, the anointed One, and His anointing. Resting in Christ, the anointed One and His anointing breaks the hold of stress and anxiety. "Therefore I say to you, do not worry about your life, what you will eat or what you will drink; nor about your body, what you will put on. Is not life more than food and the body more than clothing?" (Mathew 6:25). Worry is the enemy of faith. Worry erodes your faith and robs you the joy of anticipating God's provision.

Designed To Fight, Destined To Win

There is a famous quote that says; "There are only two things to worry about, either you are healthy or you are sick. If you are healthy, then there is nothing to worry about. But if you are sick there are only two things to worry about, either you will get well or you will die. If you get well, then there is nothing to worry about. But if you die there are only two things to worry about, either you will go to heaven or to hell. If you go to heaven, then there is nothing to worry about. And if you go to hell, you'll be so busy crying over the lost opportunities you had to repent, but which you refused to take that you won't have time to worry!"

Apply the Word of God to your life and stay out of worry and anxiety. You need to present all your worries, anxieties, and problems to God in order to let Him handle them. Give all your worries and cares to God, because He cares about what happens to you. Let your mind stay on the God without wavering.

"Casting all your care upon Him, for he cares for you" (see Peter 5:7). Cast your burden on the Lord, And He shall sustain you; He shall never permit the righteous to be moved (Psalm 55:22). "Be anxious for nothing, but in everything by prayer and supplication, with thanksgiving, let your requests be made known to God; and the peace of God, which surpasses all understanding, will guard your hearts and minds through Christ Jesus" (Philippians 4:6). "You will keep *him* in perfect peace, *Whose* mind *is* stayed *on You,* Because he trusts in You.

Guided by Wisdom

Trust in the Lord forever, For in Yah, the Lord, *is* everlasting strength" (Isaiah 26:3)

To eliminate worry from your system, you must know the reality of the Word of God. You must know who you are in Christ. You must know the reality of your redemption in Christ. You must use the authority you have in Christ. You must put on the whole amour of God. You must get into the presence of God, and you must constantly renew your mind with the Word of God. Put into practice the following points among other things discussed in this book.

1. Control your thoughts. Your thought life, not your circumstances, determines your happiness. Know who you are in Christ. Paul the Apostle teaches taught control. "Finally, brethren, whatever things are true, whatever things *are* noble, whatever things *are* just, whatever things *are* pure, whatever things *are* lovely, whatever things *are* of good report, if *there is* any virtue and if *there is* anything praiseworthy—meditate on these things" (Philippians 4:8). Peace comes when you saturate your mind with the Word of God, meditate on God's promises, and apply godly perspective in your situation. Forgive completely and totally if you have been hurt.

2. Confess all unconfessed sins. Hidden sins force uncontrolled inner frustration and separate you from the source of peace, which is God. When you are separated from the source of peace, how can you have peace? "But your iniquities have

Designed To Fight, Destined To Win

separated you from your God; And your sins have hidden *His* face from you" (Isaiah 59:2).

3. Reject bribes, greediness and gossips. "He who is greedy for gain troubles his own house, But he who hates bribes will live" (Proverb 15:27). "He who walks righteously and speaks uprightly, He who despises the gain of oppressions, Who gestures with his hands, refusing bribes, Who stops his ears from hearing of bloodshed, And shuts his eyes from seeing evil: He will dwell on high; His place of defense *will be* the fortress of rocks; Bread will be given him, His water *will be* sure."

4. Watch your mouth, and forgive. "Whoever guards his mouth and tongue Keeps his soul from troubles" (Proverbs 21:23). Forgive those who have offended you and be healed. "If anyone among you thinks he is religious, and does not bridle his tongue but deceives his own heart, this one's religion *is* useless. Pure and undefiled religion before God and the Father is this: to visit orphans and widows in their trouble, *and* to keep oneself unspotted from the world" (James 1:26).

5. Commit your ways to the Lord and trust Him. "You will keep *him* in perfect peace, *Whose* mind *is* stayed *on You,* Because he trusts in You. Trust in the Lord forever, For in Yah, the Lord, *is*

Guided by Wisdom

everlasting strength. For He brings down those who dwell on high, The lofty city; He lays it low, He lays it low to the ground, He brings it down to the dust" (Isaiah 26:3-5). Those who trust in and love God are delivered from fretting and fuming, and are given rest of soul. "Commit your way to the Lord, Trust also in Him, And He shall bring *it* to pass. He shall bring forth your righteousness as the light, And your justice as the noonday" (Psalm 37:5-6). "And my God shall supply all your need according to His riches in glory by Christ Jesus." (Philippians 4:19). The Lord is not tied to ways and means, and when one source of supplies fails you, He will open another, as He did for Elijah. "The young lions lack and suffer hunger; But those who seek the Lord shall not lack any good *thing*" (Psalm 34:10). "He who did not spare His own Son, but delivered Him up for us all, how shall He not with Him also freely give us all things?" (Romans 8:32). "And my God shall supply all your need according to His riches in glory by Christ Jesus" (Philippians 4:19). These guarantees are amply sufficient to quiet every worry and anxiety.

6. Get into the presence of the Lord. The presence of the Lord guarantees happiness, peace and joy. "In your presence is fullness of joy; at your right hand are pleasures forevermore" (Psalm 16:11). Praise the Lord all the time. There is power in

Designed To Fight, Destined To Win

your praise. When your praises goes up, the power of God comes down to your level. "Out of the mouth of babes and nursing infants You have ordained strength, because of your enemies, that you may silence the enemy and the avenger" (Psalm 8:2). **(P&P)**

61

Wisdom for LONG Life

God want you to live long on the earth. Apply the wisdom of God for long life. Determine to live your life fully to accomplish God's purpose for your life by following Gods instructions.

- Obedience to the Word of God. Obedience to God's instructions guarantees long life. "The fear of the LORD prolongs days, but the years of the wicked will be shortened" (Proverb 10:27). "But let your heart keep my commands; for length of days and long life and peace they will add to you" (Proverb 3:1). "So if you walk in My ways, to keep My statutes and My commandments, as your father David walked, then I will lengthen your days" (1 Kings 3:14). "With long life I will satisfy him, And show him My salvation" (Psalm 91:16).

Guided by Wisdom

- Obedience to parents under God's authority. Longevity is guaranteed by honor. Children, obey your parents in the Lord, for this is right. "Honor your father and mother, which is the first commandment with promise: that it may be well with you and you may live long on the earth" (Ephesians 6:1-3). "Honor your father and your mother, that your days may be long upon the land which the LORD your God is giving you" (Exodus 20:12).

- Desist from lies and deceit and seek peace. "He who would love life and see good days, Let him refrain his tongue from evil, and his lips from speaking deceit. Let him turn away from evil and do good; Let him seek peace and pursue it. For the eyes of the Lord are on the righteous, and His ears are open to their prayers. But the face of the Lord is against those who do evil" (1 Peter 3:10-12). "Who *is* the man *who* desires life, And loves *many* days, that he may see good? Keep your tongue from evil, And your lips from speaking deceit. Depart from evil and do good; Seek peace and pursue it" (Psalm 34:12-14). "Whatever good anyone does, he will receive the same from the Lord" (Ephesians 6:8).

- Walking wisely in the wisdom of God. "Hear, my son, and receive my sayings, And the years of your life will be many. I have taught you in the way of wisdom; I have led you in right paths. When you walk, your steps will not be hindered, And when you run, you will not stumble. Take firm hold of instruction, do not let go; Keep her, for she *is* your life" (Proverbs.4:10).

Designed To Fight, Destined To Win

MEDITATION

1. Forgiving is the only power that can stop the inexorable stream of painful memories.

2. Forgiveness is the attribute of the strong.

3. The weak cannot forgive. The brave and the winners rebuke and forgive, but losers play passive with unforgiveness.

4. You can forgive anything, but you cannot tolerate everything.

5. Worry is a distrust of God's providence. Worrying about the future evidences a distrust of divine providence and a doubting of God's goodness.

6. Worry does not empty tomorrow of its sorrow; it empties today of its strength.

7. Worry erodes your faith and robs you the joy of anticipating God's provision.

8. Sin pleasures today, but fatal in consequences tomorrow.

Guided by Wisdom

THE PERFECT LOVE

**Greater love has no man than this that He lay down his liife
for his friends.
For God so loved the world that He gave His one and only Son, that whoever believes in Him shall not perish but have eternal life.
(John 15:13, 3:16,NKJV)**

What account will you give when the last bell rings and the pleasure and love of sin cease to be pleasure. When you are on the brink of eternity and you find yourself standing before God alone. Do you know that heaven and hell are both real, and the choice between them is yours?

In the light of this, suppose someone cares for you and truly seeks your best interest to such an extent that He gladly exchanges His wealth for your lack, His joy for your sorrow and His life to save your life. Would you accept or reject this offer of love? I believe this is the most perfect love there is. Your answer will depend on what you think about man's sin condition.

Consequences of sin

A condition called "sin" makes one qualified for hell. Sin is anything that we do or think that is contrary to the character of God. We were all born in a sin condition before we made sin a choice. Do you have any plans to

Designed To Fight, Destined To Win

change this condition? An unchanged sin condition produces bondage and leads to hell. The bait for sin is pleasure, but the lie of sin is death. The pleasures of sin are but "for a season" (Hebrew 11:25), the aftermath is painful and not pleasant, they entail eternal torment. Sin pleasures today, but fatal in consequences tomorrow. The future state of those who reject the redemption offered to them in Jesus Christ is plainly declared to be a state of conscious, unutterable, endless torment and anguish. In Hell there are no exits. **You can't take a vacation in hell to see how you like it.** Once you are there, you are there forever! "It is appointed for men to die once, but after this the judgment" (Hebrews 9:27). It is better to die right the first time because you can't come back to do it again. What is your plan today? If you don't have a plan, the devil will give you a hell-bound plan. The devil's plan will take you to hell, but God's plan will take you to heaven.

Nothing is hidden from God

God knows your every secret sin and motives. You cannot hide anything from God. The Word of God says, "For though you wash yourself with lye, and use much soap, yet your iniquity is marked before Me, says the Lord God" (Jeremiah 2:22). "Come, see a man, who told me all things that I ever I did: Could this be the Christ." (John 4:29). It is therefore very important for you to make peace and reconcile with God through his son Jesus Christ without delay to avoid regret at last. "Times of

Guided by Wisdom

ignorance God overlooked, but now commands all men everywhere to repent" (Acts 17:30).

We have all sinned

No one except the Lord Jesus, who was the perfect Son of God, is free from the desire to sin. We were born into this world with an evil nature and with hearts that are thoroughly in love with sin. Sin is our native element. Romans 3:23 states, "All have sinned and fall short of the glory of God." Every person that has ever been born into the world comes here a sinner before God. "Wherefore, as by one man sin entered into the world, and death by sin; and so death passed upon all men, for that all have sinned" (Romans 5:12). "For all have sinned, and come short of the glory of God." (Romans. 3:23). "As it is written, There is none righteous, no, not one." (Romans. 3:10).

You are a sinner not because of the bad things you did or the bad things you are currently doing, but because of a sinful nature that you have automatically inherited. By virtue of our sin nature, we are condemned to death. Because of our sin we have been separated from God and condemned to an eternal punishment in hell. The Bible says, "For the wages of sin is death; but the gift of God is eternal life through Jesus Christ our Lord" (Romans 6:23).

Repent and be saved

To repent is to turn away from a life of sin to a life of righteousness. Repentance is a godly sorrow for sin. Repentance is revulsion of the filth and pollution of sin.

Designed To Fight, Destined To Win

Being saved means that our sins have been completely forgiven and no longer count against us. The plan of God delivers from the pleasure, love, and from the penalty or punishment of sin. Romans 4:8 states, "Blessed is the man to whom the Lord will not impute sin." Romans 3:24 states, "Being justified freely by his grace through the redemption that is in Christ Jesus." Psalm 103:12 states, "As far as the east is from the west, so far has He removed our transgressions from us."

God's plan of saving us from eternal punishment is **salvation**. Salvation is found only through Jesus Christ. Jesus Christ is a Man-God interface. He is the only mediator between man and God. Believe in Him, reject your sins, and you shall have eternal life. The Bible says, "Nor is there salvation in any other, for there is none other name under heaven given among men by which we must be saved" (Acts 4:12). "God, Who at various times and in various ways spoke in time past to the fathers by the prophets, has in these last days spoken to us by His Son, Whom He has appointed heir of all things, through Whom also He made the worlds" (Hebrews 1:1-2). "This is a faithful saying, and worthy of all acceptance, that Christ Jesus came into the world to save sinners; of whom I am chief" (1 Timothy 1:15). God knew that you could never be good enough to save yourself from sin. But He loved us so much that He did not want us to go through the terrible punishment of being separated from Him forever. So He made a plan to save us. God cares, loves, and value us so much that He sent His Son, Jesus Christ, to die to redeem us from sin. He loves us so much

Guided by Wisdom

that He gave His Son to pay the penalty for our sin. Romans 5:8 tells us, "But God demonstrates His own love toward us, in that while we were still sinners, Christ died for us."

Jesus died and was buried, but He did not stay dead. Three days later God raised Him from the dead. He died, but God was not finished with Him! God raised Jesus from the dead. Jesus defeated death, came out of the grave, spent more time on earth, and now He has rejoined His Father in Heaven. God loved His Son, but he loved us enough to allow His only Son to suffer and die as a sacrificial gift to us. God's amazing love! Without this gift that God gave us, our only choice is to die and go to a horrible place called hell and be forever eternally separated from God. In John 10:10 Jesus said: "I have come that they may have life, and that they may have it more abundantly." The last invitation of God to man says, "Let him who is thirsts come. Whoever desires let him take the water of life freely" (Revelation 22:17b).

To be saved is so very simple that it is hard for many to understand. In John 14:6 Jesus said, "I am the way, the truth, and the life. No one comes to the Father, except through Me." Through Jesus Christ, God offers you the KINGDOM OF GOD. He offers you salvation, everlasting love, and abundant life. It is written, "For God so loved the world that He gave His one and only Son, that WHOEVER believes in Him shall not perish, but have ETERNAL LIFE" (John 3:16. Emphasis added).

Designed To Fight, Destined To Win

"Behold, now is the accepted time; behold, now is the day of salvation" (2 Corinthians 6:2b).

This is a free gift. You can't buy or earn it. This gift is freely given to anybody who believes in Jesus. There is only one way to receive salvation. You must be born again by accepting Jesus Christ as your Savior. The Bible says, "Unless one is BORN AGAIN, he cannot see the kingdom of God" (John. 3:3. Emphasis added). The greatest love of all is available to you now. Men can disappoint you, but God has never disappointed any man.

The world is full of disappointments and failures. But "Jesus Christ is the same yesterday, today and forever" (Hebrews 3:8). God promised to forgive sinners, and surely He will do so (See John 3:17). For God sent not His son into the world to condemn the world; but that the world through Him might be saved. "Return to me, and I will return to you, says the Lord of hosts" (Malachi 3:7).

Today is the day of salvation, tomorrow may be too late. Jesus said, "Behold, I stand at the door and knock: if anyone hears My voice and opens the door, I will come in to him and dine with him, and he with Me" (Revelation 3:20). God is patient with man, not wanting anyone to be doomed to hell, but desiring that all would repent and be saved. **(P&P)**

<u>Guided by Wisdom</u>

PRAYER OF SALVATION

Pray the following prayer and receive Jesus as your Savior:

Dear Heavenly Father,
I come to You in the Name of Jesus. You said in your Word, "If you confess with your mouth the Lord Jesus, and believe in your heart that God has raised Him from the dead, YOU WILL BE SAVED" (Romans 10:9 Emphasis added). I believe in my heart that Jesus Christ is the Son of God. I believe He was raised from the dead for my justification. Your Word says, "With the HEART one believes unto righteousness, and with the MOUTH confession is made unto salvation" (Romans 10:10 Emphasis added). I do believe with my heart, and I confess Jesus now as my Lord. Therefore I am saved! Thank You, Father!

If you have prayed this prayer sincerely from your heart, then the Bible says you are now saved! To grow in your new Christian life, it is important to study the Bible and to pray every day to your heavenly Father. You also need to locate a good, Bible-based church where you are taught the Word of God.
The nourishment which God has provided for our spiritual growth is found in His own Word, for "Man shall not live by bread alone, but by every word that proceeds out of the mouth of God" (Mathew 4:4). It is to this that Peter has reference when he says, "As newborn babes desire the sincere (pure) milk of the Word, that ye

Designed To Fight, Destined To Win

may grow thereby" (1 Peter 2:2). In proportion as we feed upon the heavenly Manna, such will be our spiritual growth. It is equally necessary for our spiritual well-being that the old nature should be starved. This is what the apostle had in mind when he said, "Make no provision for the flesh, to *fulfill its* lusts" (Romans 13:14). To starve the old nature, to make no provision for the flesh, means that we abstain from everything that would stimulate our carnality; that we avoid, as we would a plague, all that is calculated to prove injurious to our spiritual welfare. Not only must we deny ourselves the pleasures of sin and abstain from everything upon which we cannot ask God's blessing. Our affections are to be set upon things above, and not upon things upon the earth (Colossians 3:2).

Welcome to the KINGDOM OF GOD! Write us, and let us rejoice with you. **(P&P)**

For speaking engagements, you may contact the author at:

Denalex Ministires
P.O. Box 16417
Sugar Land, Texas 77496

or

Wisdom From Above International
P.O. Box 16417
Sugar Land, Texas 77496